The Birth
and
Death of Death

Harriston L. Wilson

Foreword by Myles Munroe

*To Jeffrey + Kathy I want you to
Blessing and Peace on you and
your home + may God
richly bless you through
out the years to
come!*

MW01255061

All Scripture quotations and references are taken from the following with information used from the following sources: New King James Bible-WORDsearch 7; Jameson-Fauset-Brown Bible Commentary, WORDsearch 7, Adam Clark Commentary WORDsearch 7, Wesley's Commentary WORDsearch 7, The Message Bible, Vines Expository Dictionary, Easton's Illustrated Dictionary.

The Birth and Death of Death by Harriston L. Wilson

Library of Congress Cataloging-in-Publication
Library of Congress Control Number 2008929458

ISBN 0-9760730-64

Library of Congress Cataloging-in-Publication Data
        Wilson, Harriston L.
Printed in the United States of America

CONTENTS

Foreword

Exordium

Dedication

Acknowledgements

Preface

Introduction

FOREWORD

This erudite, eloquent, and immensely thought-provoking work gets to the heart of the deepest subject of Fear in the Human Experience on Planet earth and that's Death. The author has relied heavily on much of my work on this subject and I afforded him permission to use a major portion of my work because I wanted to share this important information with the widest market possible. He did a great job communicating this important message that affects us all.

This is indispensable reading for anyone who wants to live life above the fear of death and see it as a friend not an enemy. This is a profound authoritative work which spans the wisdom of the ages and yet breaks new ground in its approach and will possibly become a classic in this and the next generation.

This exceptional work by Harriston Wilson is one of the most profound, practical, principle-centered approaches to this very human subject I have read in a long time.

The author's approach to this ever-timely issue brings a fresh breath of air that captivates the heart, engages the mind and inspires the spirit of the reader to see death as a helpless victim rather than a victor.

The author's ability to leap over complicated theological and metaphysical jargon and reduce complex theories to simple practical principles that the least among us can understand is amazing.

This work will challenge the intellectual while embracing the laymen as it dismantles the mysterious of the soul search of mankind and delivers the profound in simplicity. Harriston's approach awakens in the reader the untapped inhibiters that retard our personal development and strips us of the life-long fear of death. His antidotes empower us to rise above these self-defeating, self-limiting factors of death to a life of exploits in spiritual and mental advancement facing the specter of death without fear.

The author also integrates into each chapter the time-tested precepts giving each principle a practical application to life making the entire process people-friendly.

Every sentence of this book is pregnant with wisdom and I enjoyed the mind-expanding experience of this exciting book. I admonish you to plunge into this ocean of knowledge and watch your life change for the better as you see death as a servant and not a conqueror of mankind.

Dr. Myles Munroe
BFM International
ITWLA
Nassau Bahamas

EXORDIUM

One of the greatest assets of any healthy, growing church is the men and women in that church who respond to a calling and carry an anointing for ministry. Even though their financial needs are met through secular employment, they see their *vocation* as the work of the Lord, in and through the local church. How tremendously hampered the ministry of every church would be if we restricted ministry to only those who fill positions on a church staff and receive a payroll check. Or if the only people allowed to "minister," were those who possess a seminary degree or some formal ministerial credential. As I consider the ministry of our own assembly, I thank God for the wonderful men and women who bring authentic, spirit-filled, life-giving, self-sacrificing ministry, from a layman's position, to every area of church life.

Harriston Wilson is such a man. Professionally, he has been an educator in the public school system, an entrepreneur and has worked in the travel industry. But through it all, he has consistently been a *man of God* whose priority is to serve the Lord through our local fellowship. His dedication has spanned decades of faithful ministry through which many have benefited. Our people honor and respect him, not because of any specific title he may carry, but because their lives have been genuinely enriched by the ministry he brings.

I was honored, as his pastor, when he asked me to consider writing this exordium to his book, which I humbly offer. Also know my goal is to not only recommend this book, but even more, to recommend the man as well. I give the author my highest recommendation. I know his heart for the Lord, I know his love for the Word of God, I know his care for the Church, and I know the character of his life.

He has chosen to take on quite a subject, as you can tell by the title, *"The Birth and Death of Death"*. It is interesting that death, for most of us, will be an unavoidable part of life, and yet it is a topic we would rather ignore or put off. After all, death is a "downer." Nobody gets excited about this dark and even fearful subject. We can come up with a plethora of things we would prefer to discuss. But let's not forget – death is the reason Jesus came in the first place. Listen, the Word didn't "become flesh" because of grace, or mercy, or faith. The "Word became flesh" because of death. Jesus said, *"The Son of Man did not come to be served, but to serve and to **give His life as a ransom for many.**"* (Mk. 10:45) He came to die, to face death and to release man from the grip death held on him.

There is much to learn about this unavoidable part of living. Fortunately, for the believer, it's Good News. In the pages of this book you will find some wonderful insights, some challenging thoughts, as well as a wealth of life changing truth taken straight from the Word of God. Open your heart – open your mind – open your Bible – and enjoy *"The Birth and Death of Death"*.

Pastor Torry Gligora,
Christian Assembly
Columbus, Ohio

DEDICATION

I extend the fondest dedication of this book to the following individuals:

To the memory of my late mother, Lucille Wilson, who taught me to seek God in all of my ways and through whose prayers I was saved. Without her foundational teachings, this book would not have been conceived.

To my beautiful wife, Gayle. Please know that you are my personal source of encouragement, inspiration and strength. You are my love and I appreciate you so much, Honey. I sincerely thank you for your patience and understanding while undertaking this task.

To the memory of my late pastor, the late Reverend Dr. Samuel Farina, who frequently encouraged me to write in the face of opposition. His constant nudging words, "Write two pages a day!" He knew that two pages would sometimes lead to ten, and then the work would be completed.

To the lovely Paulette Farina. I have had the opportunity to be a recipient of your heart felt love which is overflowing not only for our Savior, but for all of those you meet.

Special thanks to the members of Christian Assembly. I want you to know that your faithful prayers, understanding, encouraging words and loyal support were a great inspiration in writing this book.

ACKNOWLEDGEMENTS

There are many individuals who were instrumental in this work coming into fruition:

The Reverend Salvatore Gligora for taking time from his busy schedule to write the exordium;

Mike O'Ryan, the first to edit this manuscript;

Harvey Alston for his wisdom and knowledge on writing books;

Dr. Myles Munroe, thanks for his sermon on the "Birth of Death," permission to use it, and for his unsolicited foreword;

The late Reverend Dr. Samuel Farina, for all of his inspiration, encouragement, sermons and notes;

The late Dr. Richard Houston Holmes, my first pastor and mentor in the Gospel, who encouraged me to attend theology school, and to study Hebrew and Greek. He further encouraged me to research his work on the blood of Jesus;

Thomas (Mike) O'Bryan, Karen Bowen, and Ellen Queen, thank you for your edits to this manuscript.

PREFACE

The birth and death of death is a topic not often visited by many theologians. Many don't know that God has laws concerning the beginning of birth and most certainly, the finality of death. God first gives birth to (introduce) death in the Garden of Eden (Gen: 2:16-17). It is in the Garden that his spoken word gave birth to his own comments on death. God created death. God commanded the man, saying, "of every tree of the Garden thou mayest freely eat: But of the tree of the knowledge of good and evil, thou shalt not eat of it: for in the day that thou eatest thereof thou shalt surely die." God gives birth to death.

God birthed death, because He had created the world in a perfect manner. There was no need to toil. He had created plants and herbs that grew without water. All of our needs were taken care of. All we needed to do was worship him.

God birthed death as a precautionary measure for man, a warning for Adam not to step outside of God's plan. Unfortunately, Adam and Eve both stepped outside of God's plan. Their disobedience activated death as we know it today.

This book is a revelation from the Holy Spirit and compilation of authors and preachers who have spoken into my life and ministry.

- Harriston L. Wilson

INTRODUCTION

In the summer of July 2007, Dr. Myles Munroe was attending a praise and worship conference, *Exaltation*, in Columbus, Ohio. I had the pleasure and opportunity to provide transportation for him from the airport to the conference venue. During our ride to the conference center, I mentioned my writing a book, and posed a question to Dr. Munroe. "What suggestions would you give a person writing a book?" Curiously he asked, "What's your book about?" My response to him was 'The Birth and Death of Death.' Sharing with me that he had just finished preaching on the subject, he immediately suggested I get his tape.

Stunned, I could hardly believe that the author of many books had just finished preaching on the subject that God had given me the previous January! Concluding our conversation, I asked for permission to use some of his material for my book and he so graciously said, "Yes, I give you permission." Not only did he give permission, but presented me with the challenge, that if I did not write the book, he would.

I believe that God does all things on purpose and for a purpose. Therefore, the meeting with Dr. Munroe was on purpose for me. I have always been an avid student of his teachings and felt truly blessed to be able to provide transportation for him as well as share my God-inspired thoughts.

It is my sincere desire that the reader will be blessed, inspired and informed of the true meaning of the birth and death of death, and how it relates to the life of the believer.

Chapter One
My Beginning

While riding northbound on I-71 in Columbus, Ohio, I heard the words "The birth and death of death". It had been a couple of days since I had asked the Lord what to speak on for a funeral I had been called to officiate and eulogize.

[1]*"No one likes to think about death....our thoughts are of and about life. We like to think of birthdays, not death days. We like to think about graduations, weddings and anniversaries.*

When we call the family together, we would rather do so because of Thanksgiving or Christmas, not for an unplanned funeral.

We try to hold death at a distance. Death happens to others, in other places far removed from us: in

Africa, New York or on crime ridden streets, not here.

We hear about death on the news, CBS, NBC or CNN. Not here."

It was a chilly January day. Having just left the classroom, I was now on my way to a restaurant. Not in a hurry. Not feeling any sort of road rage. I was just chillin' from an average day of teaching high school. Then, out of no where, I heard a voice in my spirit say, "The birth and death of death." I thought for a moment. Where had I heard these words before? As I pondered the question, the names of a couple of my co-workers came to mind. The next day I asked them individually if they had ever heard or made such a statement. Each individual said no. Not that it really mattered, but I just thought I had heard someone say it before.

Because I had to minister at the funeral in a couple of days I began researching the topic. I carefully prepared my outline and discovered during the eulogy there was not nearly enough time to do the subject justice. Therefore, I summarized with a brief conclusion, and said, "May the Lord bless you and keep you!" It wasn't that brief, but for now that will suffice. The end, I thought! Not hardly, but, at least it was the conclusion or end for that funeral.

Prior to the funeral, my pastor, the late Dr. Samuel Farina, better known by his affectionate name "Pastor Sam", was hospitalized for a brief period of time. During his hospitalization, I had the opportunity to visit him on two different occasions. After my visitations, I decided to write a note of appreciation to him. I thought an encouraging word would be uplifting and invigorating at this time in his life.

It was during the writing of this letter (over a period of several days) that I was reading in the eighth chapter of the book of Romans when I suddenly received enlightenment from the second verse.

[2] For the law of the Spirit of life in Christ Jesus has made me free from the law of sin and death.   Romans 8:2 (NKJV)

For the first time, I recognized that there is a law governing death and within that law there exists a freedom in and from death called the Law of the Spirit of Life.

The Law of the Spirit of Life has and gives the necessary power to deliver the believer from the law of Sin and Death which, due to Adam's sin, naturally exists in man's members and conscience. The Mosaic Law brought a condemnation in that we were unable to either keep the law or overcome death. Now, after Christ came to set us free, the Spirit works in the yielding Christian the very righteousness which the Mosaic Law required.

In other words, there is a law that exists that enables man to be free from death! This is an awesome revelation that can be derived from that Scripture. I had never before received this insight while reading that passage. But any way you look at it, there is freedom in the text! There is a law, and it is the law of the Spirit of Life in Christ Jesus.

Immediately, we can see that life is the factor opposing to death! Life is the absence of death and death is the absence of life. We were dead in trespasses and sin until we were delivered (made alive) by the power of Jesus.

[1] And you *He made alive,* who were dead in trespasses and sins. Ephesians 2:1 (NKJV)

[5] even when we were dead in trespasses, made us alive together with Christ (by grace you have been saved). Ephesians 2:5 (NKJV)

[13] And you, being dead in your trespasses and the uncircumcision of your flesh, He has made alive together with Him, having forgiven you all trespasses. Colossians 2:13 (NKJV)

Resurrection has already taken place! Is there any thing in your life that has already been resurrected and you're not aware of it? If so, begin to take note. God has raised us up and made us to sit with Him in heavenly places. Yet sometimes when faced with the challenges of every day life, it is easy to forget who we are and whose we are. We must remember, 'He has the final word on life and death. And the final word on death is that it must give way to life.' Death must give way to life, think about it!

As I stated in the introduction, it was the summer of 2007 when Dr Munroe suggested I get a copy of his message on CD of the Birth of Death. Having received a CD of his message, I studied and played the information. I can only thank God for this man of God of whom God has granted a great deal of wisdom and revelation on His word. I also must add his generosity for the use of his message.

So if you find me talking or making an expression as Dr. Munroe would, you know why. Yet I have my own revelation of the birth and death of death.

Isn't it interesting that we find in the Bible that God is "The God of Abraham Isaac and Jacob." This statement could easily tell us that the reality of living the abundant life that God wanted to illustrate to mankind was too much for one man to carry. Each individual has his own personal experience and revelation. It is when we are able to view the life of Abraham's revelation, the life of Isaac's revelation along with his father's, and the life of Jacob's revelation coupled with that of his father and grandfather. We then must compile the revelations of our previous scholars in the faith.

As my pastor has said, "We should be about intergenerational ministry" It rests upon each of us to pass our encounters with God to the next generation, reconfirming the salvation experience and acts of God. Each of these individuals, Abraham, Isaac and Jacob understand a continuation of the former with the addition of an expanded awareness within their own experience.

Examining briefly, we can develop a greater awareness and image of who El Elyon is in Abraham's life. El Elyon is God the highest or most high God. Before Abraham was named Abraham he was known as Abram and experienced God as such when he delivered Lot from his capturers and was met by Melchizedek King of Salem.

[17] And the king of Sodom went out to meet him at the Valley of Shaveh (that *is,* the King's Valley), after his return from the defeat of Chedorlaomer and the kings who *were* with him.
[18] Then Melchizedek king of Salem brought out bread and wine; he *was* the priest of God Most High.
[19] And he blessed him and said: "Blessed be Abram of God Most High, Possessor of heaven and earth;
[20] And blessed be God Most High, Who has delivered your enemies into your hand." And

he   gave   him   a   tithe   of   all.
Genesis 14:17-20 (NKJV)

Abram was ninety-nine years old when the Lord appeared to him and said, "I am Almighty God" (Heb. El Shaddai). This revelation of God brings not only enrichment but creates fruitfulness in Abram's life at a time when there was no fruit.

The Lord asks a question in Gen 18:14,

"Is anything too hard for the Lord?"

Now, it's laughing time when a man who is one year shy of one hundred years old and his wife ten years his junior is talking about having a baby.
He-he, ha-ha, but the revelation that Abraham learned and that we must learn is that nothing, absolutely nothing, is too hard for the Lord. From death to life, now or later, God can bring that thing that is dead in your body to life again. He can do it now or later.

In Abraham's case He chose the now. From death to life Abraham and Sarah experienced a physical enablement (a miracle) unlike that of a hundred year-old man and a ninety year-old woman. In the absence of viagra, levitra, cialis, ascend, passion-Rx, or extenze, they only had A.M.G. - All Mighty God. With A.M.G., Sarah was once again birthed into a life of enjoyable pleasurable romance with her husband. Notice her question:

> [12] Therefore Sarah laughed within herself, saying, "After I have grown old, shall I have pleasure, my lord being old also?"
> [13] And the Lord said to Abraham, "Why did Sarah laugh, saying, 'Shall I surely bear *a child,* since I am old?'
> [14] Is anything too hard for the Lord? At the appointed time I will return to you, according to the time of life, and Sarah shall have a son."
>
> Genesis 18:12-14 (NKJV)

What an experience and revelation, quickening the dead, resurrection power, from death to life again. From dead cells to a vibrant embryo suggest shouts of joy. I believe Sarah said at the least 'Amen.'

Married women, today if your desire is to have a child, I want you to know that the A.M.G. is the same today as He was yesterday. You have the A.M.G. in you. The greater One lives in you! If your marriage is dead, no fun, no humor, that is not God's abundant life for you.

Now let's look at Isaac's revelation. Isaac, a type of Christ, means 'obedient unto death'

[7] But Isaac spoke to Abraham his father and said, "My father!" And he said, "Here I am, my son." Then he said, "Look, the fire and the wood, but where *is* the lamb for a burnt offering?"
[8] And Abraham said, "My son, God will provide for Himself the lamb for a burnt offering." So the two of them went together. Genesis 22:7-8 (NKJV)

Father and son will experience God as Jehovah-Jireh, my provider.

[13] Then Abraham lifted his eyes and looked, and there behind *him was* a ram caught in a thicket by its horns. So Abraham went and took the ram, and offered it up for a burnt offering instead of his son.
[14] And Abraham called the name of the place, The-Lord-Will-Provide; as it is said *to* this day, "In the Mount of The Lord it shall be provided." Genesis 22:13-14 (NKJV)

Here we see the God who anticipates our need in advance and provides. The ram did not just fall out of the sky, but at some point the ram left the herd maybe prior to Abraham and Isaac's arrival and was caught in the thicket. Similarly, the Lord, Jehovah-Jireh, has already made provision for your journey.

Upon Isaac's return to Beer-sheba, the Lord made himself known.

^{23} Then he went up from there to Beer-Sheba. ^{24} And the Lord appeared to him the same night and said, "I *am* the God of your father Abraham; do not fear, for I *am* with you. I will bless you and multiply your descendants for My servant Abraham's sake." Genesis 26:23-24 (NKJV)

Now after Isaac had his father's blessing confirmed in his own life, he then realized that he had the ability to bless his own sons and did so. In his statement affirming the blessing on Jacob he says, "yea, and he shall be blessed."

^{33} Then Isaac trembled exceedingly, and said, "Who? Where *is* the one who hunted game and brought *it* to me? I ate all *of it* before you , and I have blessed him--*and* indeed he shall be   blessed." ^{34} When Esau heard the words of his father, he cried with an exceedingly great and bitter cry, and said to his father, "Bless me--me also,   O   my   father!" Genesis 27:33-34 (NKJV)

It's Jacob's turn now. Although he steals his brother Esau's blessing, he will still be blessed. Isaac confirms a blessing from Abraham upon Jacob.

> [3] "May God Almighty bless you, And make you fruitful and multiply you, That you may be an assembly of peoples; [4] And give you the blessing of Abraham, To you and your descendants with you, That you may inherit the land in which you are a stranger, Which God gave to Abraham." [5] So Isaac sent Jacob away, and he went to Padan Aram, to Laban the son of Bethuel the Syrian, the brother of Rebekah, the mother of Jacob and Esau.
> Genesis 28:3-5 (NKJV)

Jacob at Haran becomes a striking illustration of us who sometimes leaves the place of blessing, yet God will retain his hand of mercy and grace upon our life.

Working over time for a wife in a strange land, he was deceived, yet under the covenant care of Jehovah. Not the best life one can have.

[8] Keep a cool head. Stay alert.
The Devil is poised to pounce, and
would like nothing better than to
catch you napping.
1 Peter 5:8 (MSG)

Chapter Two
The Garden

The law of life has been compromised by the law of sin and death. When sin and death entered the picture in the garden after Adam refused to obey God, He relinquished the law of life thus permitting death.

> [16] And the Lord God commanded the man, saying, "Of every tree of the garden you may freely eat;
>
> [17] but of the tree of the knowledge of good and evil you shall not eat, for in the day that you eat of it you shall surely die." Genesis 2:16-17 (KJV)

Sin is rebellion against God. It also means to miss the mark. For the philosopher, sin is the improper attitude toward a known obligation. For the layman, sin is being out of the will and favor of God. In simple terms you messed up, you blew it, you missed it.

Man was made in the image of God and possessed the purest form of life, but because he refused to follow simple directions, 'don't eat of the fruit of the tree of the knowledge of good and evil,' he opened himself and his descendents to the law of sin and death.

> [1] Now the serpent was more cunning than any beast of the field which the Lord God had made. And he said to the woman, "Has God indeed said, 'you shall not eat of every tree of the garden'?" Genesis 3:1 (NKJV)

Satan begins by planting a seed of doubt about God's word. While pondering his tactics, Eve tries to match wits with him.

> [2] And the woman said to the serpent, "We may eat the fruit of the trees of the garden;
>
> [3] but of the fruit of the tree which *is* in the midst of the garden, God has said,

'You shall not eat it, nor shall you touch it, lest you die. "

⁴ Then the serpent said to the woman, "You will not surely die. Genesis 3:2-4 (NKJV)

Don't try it! Resist him by using the word in 1 Peter 5:8-9; James 4:7.

⁸ Be sober, be vigilant; because your adversary the devil walks about like a roaring lion, seeking whom he may devour.

⁹ Resist him, steadfast in the faith, knowing that the same sufferings are experienced by your brotherhood in the world.
1 Peter 5:8-9 (NKJV)

⁷ Therefore submit to God. Resist the devil and he will flee from you. James 4:7 (NKJV)

Satan ends by denying God's Word.

⁵ For God knows that in the day you eat of it your eyes will be opened and you

will be like God, knowing good and
evil."

[6] So when the woman saw that the tree
was good for food,

Lust of the flesh
and that it was pleasant to the eyes,

Lust of the eyes
and a tree desirable to make one wise,

Pride of life
she took of its fruit and ate. She also
gave to her husband with her, and he
ate.   Genesis 3:5-6 (NKJV)

[7] Then the eyes of both of them were
opened, and they knew that they were
naked; and they sewed fig leaves
together and made themselves
coverings.   Genesis 3:7 (NKJV)

Their eyes were open and they knew good
and evil, but not as God did. Thus a half truth
presented as a whole truth is an untruth.
    God wanted Adam to know only good and
not experience evil, but instead he now would
discover what the evil was and what the good would
have been!

Often experience is not the best teacher, for sometimes the tuition is too expensive!

[8] And they heard the sound of the Lord God walking in the garden in the cool of the day, and Adam and his wife hid themselves from the presence of the Lord God among the trees of the garden.

[9] Then the Lord God called to Adam and said to him, "Where are you?"

[10] So he said, "I heard Your voice in the garden, and I was afraid because I was naked; and I hid myself."

Genesis 3:8-10 (NKJV)

After the call of God to Adam, Adam's response was, I heard you, but I was afraid. What was he afraid of? They had walked and talked prior to this moment and now Adam is fearful. Here begins the age long process of man hiding himself from his maker. He said, "I was afraid because I was naked." Now we see the immediate consequences of sin. It could very well be described as shame. The same shame a little child would display as an attitude of one who has disobeyed and is now uncomfortable standing in the presence of their parents.

I hid myself because I rebelled against your word and cannot face you. Adam is fearful and hiding because he has now recognized that they had been deceived by the serpent and are now being exposed to death and punishment by God.

This attempt of Adam to hide himself from God is the ultimate tragic result of sin. Sin not only separates man from God, but makes him actually afraid to approach or face God.

Unfortunately, there is no confession on Adam's part. There is no effort to make amends for his rebellion. Like Adam, there is great difficulty in approaching God when there is no covering for sin. We need to be covered and clothed with the righteousness of Christ, and then we can approach God openly, freely and boldly.

Chapter Three
The Birth of Death

If we were to look at two different scenarios of the birth of death we would find the following.

First the birth of death can be traced back to Genesis 2:16-17:

> [16] And the Lord God commanded the man, saying, "Of every tree of the garden you may freely eat;

> [17] but of the tree of the knowledge of good and evil you shall not eat, for in

the day that you eat of it you shall surely die." Genesis 2:16-17 (NKJV)

The Message Bible has a unique revealing and direct presentation of the story.

[16] God commanded the Man, "You can eat from any tree in the garden,

[17] except from the Tree-of-Knowledge-of-Good-and-Evil. Don't eat from it. The moment you eat from that tree, you're dead."
Genesis 2:16-17 (MSG)

[2]"thou shalt not eat of it . . . thou shalt surely die -- no reason assigned for the prohibition,   but death was to be the punishment of   disobedience. A positive command like this   was not only the simplest and easiest, but the only trial to which their fidelity could be   exposed."

Of all the books and research on birth and death, I could not find one with these subject married. I found birth to death and each alone but not together. But I like what Dr. Myles Munroe says and I quote:

[3]"This is the first time in the Bible that the word die/death shows up and it is introduced by God, not Satan."

"It is God that is talking in this chapter and this word 'die' is an invention of God. Therefore, it could be said that God created death."

"It has been long thought that death was created and designed by Satan, but that is not the case. Let me suggest that God created death. In this chapter, there is no Satan, no devil, no demons, no darkness. In this chapter, there is God and God is talking to man and God says to man, "the day you eat you shall surely die." Die is introduced by God, so death is something that God created and he introduced it to Adam."

"God created death, told Adam about it, and then He told Adam death has no power. He explains: the trees, the tree of the knowledge of good and evil, and death. He continues to say as long as you don't touch that tree, death can not kill you. But if you eat from that tree, the tree of the knowledge of good and evil, if you disobey My commandments, if you break My Word, then that thing that I made that has no power will suddenly come alive and it will kill you."

"In other words, death existed before it killed. Death was present, but it could not kill Adam as long as Adam did not disobey God."

"God created death without power and the only way death could get power to kill was from

Adam when he disobeyed God. So as long as Adam obeyed God death was helpless, hopeless, powerless and dead. Let me suggest that death was created dead."

From that quote we see that, death had no life. It could not kill the man Adam. It was there, but it had no power. Death had no power and no life.

In life, we constantly walk through the valley of the shadow of death, but at the same time death cannot just come up and take our life. Death is still powerless until given birth through disobedience to God's word.

> [3] He restores my soul; He leads me in the paths of righteousness For His name's sake.

> [4] Yea, though I walk through the valley of the shadow of death, I will fear no evil; For You are with me; Your rod and Your staff, they comfort me. Psalms 23:3-4 (NKJV)

As we walk in righteousness, we need not fear death. Death is good. Death kills God's enemies. Death kills and will kill the enemies of God and man.

God created everything and when God finished his creation, He said this was good. So, death is good when it has no power.

What is so good about death when it has no power? It can't kill you! The most horrific nightmare that death could ever have is to be able to kill.

Dr. Myles Munroe says "Death was created not to kill, and that is when it is in its good state. Death when it is given power is abnormal. Death cannot kill without permission and when death kills it is abnormal. Death in its normal state has no power to kill." Note: **Death is a judgement.**

Secondly, if we were to define death as separation from God, we could trace its original birthing with Satan as he was cast out of heaven.

Note Isaiah 14:11-17:

[11] Your pomp is brought down to Sheol, *And* the sound of your stringed instruments; The maggot is spread under you, And worms cover you.'

[12] "How you are fallen from heaven, O Lucifer, son of the morning! How you are cut down to the ground, You who weakened the nations!

[13] For you have said in your heart: 'I will ascend into heaven, I will exalt my

throne above the stars of God; I will also sit on the mount of the congregation on the farthest sides of the north;

[14] I will ascend above the heights of the clouds; I will be like the Most High.'

[15] Yet you shall be brought down to Sheol, to the lowest depths of the Pit.

[16] "Those who see you will gaze at you, *And* consider you, *saying:* '*Is* this the man who made the earth tremble, Who shook kingdoms,

[17] Who made the world as a wilderness and destroyed its cities, *who* did not open the house of his prisoners?'

Although some theologians and commentaries say that this is referring to the King of Babylon and how he was remarkably brought down and triumphed over, others give this passage of Scripture a primary spiritual meaning as to the fall of Satan from heaven. Jesus said in Luke that he saw Satan fall like lightning from heaven.

¹⁷ Then the seventy returned with joy, saying, "Lord, even the demons are subject to us in Your name."

¹⁸ And He said to them, "I saw Satan fall like lightning from heaven.

¹⁹ Behold, I give you the authority to trample on serpents and scorpions, and over all the power of the enemy, and nothing shall by any means hurt you.

²⁰ Nevertheless do not rejoice in this, that the spirits are subject to you, but rather rejoice because your names are written in heaven."

Luke 10:17-20 (NKJV)

J. Vernon McGee says it like this:

⁴"Lucifer" is none other than Satan. Lucifer, according to Ezekiel 28, is the highest creature that God ever created. But he was a Judas Iscariot -- he turned on God. He set his will over God's will. In Luke 10:18, the Lord Jesus says, ". . . I beheld Satan as lightning fall from heaven." In 1 John 3:8, we are told, "He that committeth sin is of the devil; for the devil sinneth from the beginning.

It is interesting to note here that Jesus not only mentions the fall of Satan, the supreme adversary, falling as lightning with the utmost suddenness, but gives his disciples power over this tyrant and all the power that he possesses. Did you notice, ALL THE POWER? We can surmise that all our victories over Satan are obtained by power derived from Jesus Christ.

By this fall of Satan to the earth and the deception of the man and woman (Adam and Eve) in the earth by way of the serpent, the gene of depravity descended throughout the Adamic posterity making us all sinners from birth and subject to physical and spiritual death. Being born in sin and alienated from God, we need a savior, Jesus Christ, to bridge the gap and restore our relationship with Father God.

The following commentaries deal with death in the following manner:

[2]Jamieson-Fausset-Brown Bible Commentary says, "Thou shalt not eat of it . . . thou shalt surely die. No reason assigned for the prohibition, but death was to be the punishment of disobedience. A positive command like this was not only the simplest and easiest, but the only trial to which their fidelity could be exposed."

Adam Clarke's Commentary gives this light on the subject, [5]"Thou shalt surely die— מות

תמות moth tamuth". Literally, a death thou shalt die; or, dying thou shalt die. Thou shalt not only die spiritually, by losing the life of God, but from that moment thou shalt become mortal, and shalt continue in a dying state till thou die. This we find literally accomplished; every moment of man's life may be considered as an act of dying, till soul and body are separated. Other meanings have been given of this passage, but they are in general either fanciful or incorrect."

[6]Wesley's Commentary shares this view, "Thou shall die. That is, thou shalt lose all the happiness thou hast either in possession or prospect; and thou shalt become liable to death, and all the miseries that preface and attend it. This was threatened as the immediate consequence of sin."

"In the day thou eatest, thou shalt die - Not only thou shalt become mortal, but spiritual death and the forerunners of temporal death shall immediately seize thee."

I kneel in worship facing your holy temple and say it again: "Thank you!" Thank you for your love, thank you for your faithfulness; Most holy is your name, most holy is your Word.
Psalms 138:2 (MSG)

Chapter Four
Three Deaths

L et us consider death as a three-fold or three level experience. Dr. Myles Munroe explains three deaths as follows:

[3]"First, death is the departure of the Holy Spirit from the spirit of man. This is the most dangerous level of death.

May I suggest to you, according to the Word of God that the first level of death is the one God is really concerned about. But death is progressive. When Adam first sinned, the Bible says "The day you eat you shall surely die." That means the day Adam and Eve picked and ate that fruit and broke God's word, according to God, they died!

The very day Adam sinned, he died. That means, if Adam lived according to the Bible nine hundred and thirty years after he picked the fruit, then according to God, physical dying is not the primary death.

"The day Adam ate he died, but he lived physically nine hundred and thirty years, as recorded in the Bible. In other words, Adam was a dead living man.

What does that mean? It means the moment Adam sinned, broke God's word, rebelled against God, missed the mark, the Holy Spirit left Adam's spirit and Adam became dead to God.

Therefore, the ultimate aspect of death is the departure of the Holy Spirit of God. This is the eternal death. When the Holy Spirit left, due to the disobedience of man, death was made alive.

A man without the Holy Spirit is a dead man. He may have a three piece suit and be well-dressed, but he is just a well-dressed dead man. The athlete who wins the gold metal and does not have the Holy Spirit, is a dead man to God. You see, it does not matter what you accomplish. If you don't have the Holy Spirit inside of you, you are just a successful dead man.

Adam was dead the day he died before God and the Holy Spirit left him. Yet, he lived nine hundred and thirty years and the Bible says he had children.

Dead people do have children. The only problem is the Bible says he produced after his own kind."

> And Adam lived one hundred and thirty years, and begot a son in his own likeness, after his image.
>
> Genesis 5:3 (NKJV)

[3]"This means dead people produce dead people, who produce dead people, who produce dead people. That means your new born baby is born dead.

At the second level, death is the departure of man from the presence of God. Death was never God's will for mankind. We should never think that God created man to kill him. God told Adam death is present but it has no power. Death to Adam was a choice. God did not kill Adam, death killed him.

Death did not choose to kill Adam. Adam chose to be killed by death. God told Adam, "Death is present but it has no power. It's up to you! If you disobey my word, the death that has no power will suddenly be given life and kill you from the life it got from your disobedience."

Therefore, death was given birth when Adam disobeyed God. Death was created by God and it had no life at all until it was given power by the disobedience of man.

When Adam sinned, he was removed from the presence of God. His removal from the garden was a physical representation of a spiritual reality. He himself fled from the presence of God."

> [8] And they heard the sound of the Lord God walking in the garden in the cool of the day, and Adam and his wife hid themselves from the presence of the Lord God among the trees of the garden.
>
> [9] Then the Lord God called to Adam and said to him, "Where *are* you?"
>
> [10] So he said, "I heard Your voice in the garden, and I was afraid because I was naked; and I hid myself."   Genesis 3:8-10 (NKJV)
>
> [23] therefore the Lord God sent him out of the garden of Eden to till the ground from which he was taken.
>
> [24] So He drove out the man; and He placed cherubim at the east of the Garden of Eden, and a flaming sword which turned every way, to guard the way to the tree of life.
>   Genesis 3:23-24 (NKJV)

[3]"In the third level of death, death is the departure of man's spirit and soul from his physical body. This is considered physical death and the one with which we are most familiar. However, it is this physical death that transfers us from the physical realm to the spiritual realm. In the spiritual realm, we are alive and well if we have accepted the Lord as our Savior during our earthly life. If there is no acceptance of Christ in the earthly life, then there is living hell after physical death.

So we have three aspects called death. Death when the Holy Spirit left man's spirit, death when man is driven from the presence of God, and death when man leaves his body, because his body is rotting under the sting of sin.

It was not God's original intention for man to die. You see, man has a free will, and privilege always creates responsibility. The man who is given a free will must be given a test to determine whether he will obey God or not.

Man is a triune being, and he would have to die in a threefold way. Adam did not die physically until over nine hundred years after his fall, but God said, "In the day you eat, you shall die." Death means separation, and Adam was separated from God spiritually the very day he ate, you may be sure of that."

14b By embracing death, taking it into himself, he destroyed the Devil's hold on death 15 and freed all who cower through life, scared to death of death. Hebrews 2:14b-15 (MSG)

Chapter Five

"I Am" My Name

The curse of death is the ultimate result of disobedience. It's the rebellion of man against God that caused death. And God calls it sin.

The word sin when it refers to Jesus is usually a singular word. It very rarely says that he died for our sins (plural). It usually says in the Scripture that He died for our sin (singular).

It is singular in the Greek and Hebrew, because He really died for only one sin, the sin of rebellion against God.

The word sin in the Hebrew language is the word rebellion. The word sin in the New Testament Greek is not only rebellion, but it also means to miss the mark. This is what man did. God pronounced the curse of death upon man.

The scripture shows the pronouncement.

[16] And the Lord God commanded the man, saying, "Of every tree of the garden you may freely eat;

[17] but of the tree of the knowledge of good and evil you shall not eat, for in the day that you eat of it you shall surely die." Genesis 2:16-17 (NKJV)

What was the curse? It was the curse that God told him. "Adam the day you eat from this tree, you shall surely die." Surely means 'I will make sure.' In other words, I swear you will die! This word surely is God taking responsibility to make sure that death does its job if Adam disobeys God's word. 'If you break my law, Adam, I personally must make sure that you die.'

One of the greatest mysteries is the life that death has. Let's look at it. Man's sin gave life and power to death.

[12] Therefore, just as through one man sin entered the world, and death through sin, and thus death spread to all men, because all sinned. *Notice death by sin.*

¹³ For until the law sin was in the world, but sin is not imputed when there is no law

¹⁴ Nevertheless, death reigned from Adam to Moses, even over those who had not sinned according to the likeness of the transgression of Adam, who is a type of Him who was to come. Romans 5:12-14 (NKJV)

Notice that man's sin brought death. Death came through sin. The Bible says death came through sin. In other words, death did not come through the man; it came through the act of the man. Death is a product of sin.

Because God is the great "I Am", Dr. Munroe suggests two reasons man had to die.

³"The first reason is because **God is Holy.** The word holy means pure in motive. It also means integrated or to be one with yourself. Holy means what you say and what you do are one. Holy means you don't say one thing and do another. Holy means whatever you say, you do, and whatever you do is what you said. Holy then means to be integrated or to have integrity. God cannot say one thing and then do another."

"When God told Adam, 'The day you eat you shall surely die', God had to make sure it happened."

Because what he says, and what he does are the same.

"A second reason is, because *God is faithful.* God had to make sure man died because He is faithful. He is faithful to himself. Because God cannot lie, he has to kill man."

> [1] Paul, a bondservant of God and an apostle of Jesus Christ, according to the faith of God's elect and the acknowledgment of the truth which accords with godliness,
>
> [2] in hope of eternal life which God, who cannot lie, promised before time began. Titus 1:1-2

"God cannot say one thing and do another. When God told Adam the day you eat you shall surely die, is what he meant. God had to make sure Adam died to make sure He was faithful to His word, and that He did not lie."

"Because God cannot lie, He has to kill man or make sure that death does. God MUST keep His word. The killing of man was the faithfulness of God in action."

He also must keep His own promise. His Word is His promise, and His promises are His Word.

We like the promises of God when he says he promises to bless us, to save us, but He also promised to kill us. When God spoke to Adam, and said if you eat this fruit, you are dead, it's a promise just like any other.

When man was disobedient in eating the fruit, the Holy Spirit left, Adam was kicked out of the garden, separated from God and his body began to deteriorate. God said (author's liberty), It was my Word and I cannot lie. You sinned and you died.

Look at Psalm 138:2

> [2] I will worship toward Your holy temple, And praise Your name For Your loving-kindness and Your truth; For You have magnified Your word above all Your name.

God has exalted His Word above everything. God says He has placed His word above His name. The Hebrew word for name is the same word as being. That is why in Hebrew when you name something, it is the thing that you name it.

In Exodus when Moses asked God his name,

> [11] And Moses said unto God, Who am I, that I should go unto Pharaoh, and

that I should bring forth the children of Israel out of Egypt?

[12] And he said, certainly I will be with thee; and this shall be a token unto thee, that I have sent thee: When thou hast brought forth the people out of Egypt, ye shall serve God upon this mountain.

[13] And Moses said unto God, Behold, when I come unto the children of Israel, and shall say unto them, The God of your fathers hath sent me unto you; and they shall say to me, what *is* his name? What shall I say unto them?

[14] And God said unto Moses, I AM THAT I AM: and He said, Thus shalt thou say unto the children of Israel, I AM hath sent me unto you.

[15] And God said moreover unto Moses, Thus shalt thou say unto the children of Israel, The LORD God of your fathers, the God of Abraham, the God of Isaac, and the God of Jacob, hath sent me unto you: this *is* my name for ever, and this *is* my memorial unto all generations.   Exodus 3:11-15 (NKJV)

I AM THAT I AM constitutes the idea that God is the Being who is absolutely self-existent. God within himself possesses essential life and existence. In the Hebrew it not only means to exist but to be active, to express oneself in active being. The "I AM" or "I WILL BE" is God's promise that he will redeem Israel and, in the future, mankind. We as the children of Israel want to be assured that he will meet us in our time of need and deliver proving His character and promises.

[10] "But you are my witnesses." God's Decree. "You're my handpicked servant So that you'll come to know and trust me, understand both that I am and who I am. Previous to me there was no such thing as a god, nor will there be after me.

[11] I, yes I am God. I'm the only Savior there is.

[12] I spoke, I saved, I told you what existed long before these upstart gods appeared on the scene. And you know it, you're my witnesses, you're the evidence." God's Decree. "Yes, I am God.

[13] I've always been God and I always will be God. No one can take anything from me. I make; who can unmake it?"
Isaiah 43:10-13 (MSG)

God had to reply, "I am," is my name", because in Hebrew name means to be. In other words, the thing is its name. When God says I have placed my Word above my name, He is literally saying I have placed my word above myself. In other words when I speak I too must be under my own words and do it. God will never speak a word that He himself must not obey. He placed His word above His name. As Dr. Munroe puts it, "God is sovereign until He speaks."

God is sovereign as long as he doesn't talk. When he speaks, He is no longer sovereign. That word becomes His regulator. That is why God says, He will move heaven and earth before one letter of His Word doesn't come to pass. He says His word is established for ever.

That means when God told Adam the day you eat you will surely die, God was setting up a system of authority that says if you disobey me you give life to death. Because I cannot break my word death will have to kill you, Adam, and all of your descendants that you are carrying.

Again in Romans 5:12-14

[12] Therefore, just as through one man sin entered the world, and death through sin, and thus death spread to all men, because all sinned.

[13] For until the law sin was in the world, but sin is not imputed when there is no law.

[14] Nevertheless, death reigned from Adam to Moses, even over those who had not sinned according to the likeness of the transgression of Adam, who is a type of Him who was to come.
Romans 5:12-14 (NKJV)

Man had to die, because God must keep his Word. God is holy, faithful, and cannot lie. All the promises God has made, He will fulfill, because He cannot ignore his word.

Why did Jesus come? Why did He have to die? Why could He not have just spoken a word from heaven and redeemed mankind? Let's look at a eight possible reasons.

1. Substitution. He had to die because something had to die.

2. The flesh. God had to become a man in order for Him to save man.

3. Blood. He had to die, because God required a blood sacrifice.

> [11] For the life of the flesh is in the blood, and I have given it to you upon the altar to make atonement for your souls; for it is the blood that makes atonement for the soul.
>
> Leviticus 17:11 (NKJV)

> [14] Inasmuch then as the children have partaken of flesh and blood, He Himself likewise shared in the same, that through death He might destroy him who had the power of death, that is, the devil.   Hebrews 2:14 (NKJV)

Man does not have a spirit; he is a spirit. Man never really dies. That's why if you die without knowing Christ, you still live forever. The Bible calls it eternal death, because you are a spirit. If you die in Christ, then you are raised by Him and you live forever and that is called eternal life.

Don't think for once that when you die without Christ in your life and you go to the grave, there is no problem; neither when the judgment day comes there is no problem. Nor when you stand before God and are judged, no problem. This is just the threshold of the problem. When you are judged and sent you into eternal suffering, that's the problem. Why? Because eternal life is for eternity which means forever and ever. That means the problem is you will not burn up. You will burn as the worm that does not die.

You will not burn up because you are a spirit. Jesus said when you are cast into hell, the fire never quenches and the worm does not die and there is weeping and gnashing of teeth. This is forever and ever, throughout eternity.

[44] where *'Their worm does not die, And the fire is not quenched.'*

[45] And if your foot causes you to sin, cut it off. It is better for you to enter life lame, rather than having two feet, to be cast into hell, into the fire that shall never be quenched--

[46] where *'Their worm does not die, And the fire is not quenched.'*

[47] And if your eye causes you to sin, pluck it out. It is better for you to enter the kingdom of God with one eye, rather than having two eyes, to be cast into hell fire.
Mark 9:44-47 (NKJV)

Verses 44 and 46 are not in some manuscripts. However, we are talking about eternal death. It is Hell in laymen's terms.

Man as a spirit, cannot die. But God needed death. Remember the three kinds of death: the Holy Spirit leaving man, then man is removed from the presence of God, and lastly the spirit leaving the body.

Now in order for God to solve the problem He must get out of the spirit realm, because a spirit cannot die. He must be born of a woman who will provide a body for him and he will then be able to become a candidate for death. 'For without the shedding of blood there is no remission of sin. He then must die the same three deaths as man.

On what we call Good Friday, Christ was on the cross. Before they arrested Him, He was in the garden praying and he said, "Let this cup, (The word cup means redemptive price) pass from me."

Some say the cup was the cross, but that does not mean the suffering of death. The cup was that He was made sin for us. Another theologian might say while the cup may refer to death, it is more likely that the cup represents the wrath of God against sin, the divine wrath Christ would incur on the cross as man's sin bearer. Thus, Christ died a substitutionary death for mankind.

In other words, 'is there any other way to do this? Nevertheless, not my will but thy will be done.'

As He approached the cross, they whipped him, they stripped Him, they put nails in His hands, and they hung Him on the cross.

Now in order to be a substitute he must experience the exact death that you and I experience. First, He must die by the Holy Spirit leaving him. Second, He must die by being removed from the presence of God, and thirdly, He must die by His spirit leaving His body.

Dr. Munroe says the following: [3]"Let's see if He did it! On the cross, Jesus begins to talk and He talks through each death. First he asks, "Father, why have you forsaken me?"

This is His fourth cry from the cross and is directed to the father, we see this also in Psalms 22.

"For one brief moment God left God. He had never felt what it was like to be away from His father. He is now experiencing being out of the presence of Father."

"He tasted. (Heb. 2:9) He couldn't live there so he just tasted the absence for three days. The Bible says he screamed out. Imagine Jesus screaming, but when you are out of the presence of God, you do strange things. When you are out of Eden you mal-function, kill your brother, sister, mother. We see it in our newspapers today. Children out of Eden out of God's presence do dumb things. That's why we have crime. Crime is man out of God's presence.

And Christ tasted what it meant to be out of God's presence." "Then the Bible says he cried out, "I thirst."

> [28] After this, Jesus, knowing that all things were now accomplished, that the Scripture might be fulfilled said, "I thirst!" John 19:28 (NKJV)

They then tried to give him a mixture that they used to kill pain. The Bible says he refused it. In other words, they tried to give him a pain killer made of hyssop and herbs. But he refused it; he refused it because he had to carry our pain in his own body. That is why if you are sick and hurting today you can say, God, this pain is not legal. The pain you may feel in your body has no rights, because He carried our pain."

The only words Jesus spoke indicating pain or discomfort were, "I thirst." It was not that He did not suffer, but He did not complain. This fifth statement on the cross indicates that He did without doubt carry our pain. We can thank God today and be free from continual pain in our body.

That's a reason to praise God right now, where ever you are! If He had taken that pain killer, you would have a right to keep your pain.

Please note, the difference in the wine mixed with myrrh in Matthew 27:34 and Mark 15:23, that

He refused to drink, and the vinegar in John 19:28 which he did drink for thirst.

The wine mixed with myrrh was given to malefactors at the place of execution, to intoxicate them, and make them less sensible to pain. Christ, therefore, with great propriety, refused the aid of such remedies.

In Matthew 27:34, they gave Him sour wine mingled with gall (wine mixed with myrrh) to drink. But when He had tasted it, He would not drink.

> [5] *"A vessel full of vinegar* was probably that tart wine which we are assured was the common drink of the Roman soldiers. Our word vinegar comes from the French vin aigre, sour or tart wine; and, although it is probable that it was brought at this time for the use of the four Roman soldiers who were employed in the crucifixion of our Lord, it is as probable that it might have been furnished for the use of the persons crucified; who, in that lingering kind of death, must necessarily be grievously tormented with thirst. This vinegar must not be confounded with the vinegar and gall mentioned in Matthew 27:34, and Mark 15:23. That, being a stupefying portion,

intended to alleviate his pain, he refused to drink; but of this he took a little, and then expired, John 19:30." Adam Clarke's Commentary

[28] After this, Jesus, knowing that all things were now accomplished, that the Scripture might be fulfilled, said, "I thirst!"

[29.] Now a vessel full of sour wine was sitting there; and they filled a sponge with sour wine, put *it* on hyssop, and put *it* to His mouth.

[30.] So when Jesus had received the sour wine, He said, "It is finished!" And bowing His head, He gave up His spirit. John 19:28-30 (NKJV)

It is suggested He gave up the Holy Spirit. The Holy Spirit is now leaving the body.

Dr. Munroe states, "Then the Bible says He gave up the ghost which means He gave up the Holy Ghost. Death means to loose the Holy Ghost or Holy Spirit. The Spirit of God was gone, and then He bowed his head and died."

Let's look at it again. He was forsaken by God, God's presence left Him. He gave up the ghost. The Spirit of God gone, but He is still there.

Now, notice what He did. He bowed his head. He is now leaving the body.

He died completely, not for himself, but for us. He substituted himself. He paid death its due. That's why we must surrender all to Him, because we owe it (our life) all to Him.

> [14.] In as much then as the children have partaken of flesh and blood, He Himself likewise shared in the same, that through death He might destroy him who had the power of death, that is, the devil. Hebrews 2:14 (NKJV)

He shared or took part. The part He took from man is flesh. He did not take the blood of man. His blood is sinless. His blood was generated by way of the Holy Spirit.

Life and death is in the blood. If you want death, it's in the blood. If you want life, it's in the blood. Spirits have no blood. God had to have Jesus supply the blood.

That's why we worship Jesus. We don't worship Him to try to make Him a God. He is God, all by Himself. He is the body of God. He is the vessel that God used to carry out the blood sacrifice. That is why Jesus said this cup is the blood of my covenant, drink it.

Now, observing more reasons Jesus had to die.

4. He also had to die because sin had to be paid for.

5. He died because He had to be made sin for us. Only by having sin thrust upon Him.

6. He had to die because he had to be resurrected. You cannot resurrect living things. You only resurrect dead things.

7. He had to die to justify us. That means he had to die to satisfy the demands of righteousness.

8. He had to die to destroy the power of death. He had to put death back to sleep. Death dies when it kills you.

Oral Roberts said, "The ultimate healing is death." When you get healed by death, you can't get sick any more! Death is dead where you are concerned.

Death can be a blessing, because when death is activated, it cannot kill you anymore.

In Psalms 116:15 we read:

[15] Precious in the sight of the LORD is the death of his saints. Psalms 116:15 (KJV)

Beautiful in the eyes of the Lord is the death of his saints. Why? Suggestion: Because death no longer has any power.

When death kills, it looses its power. Once death kills something, it can't kill it anymore. If God can get death to kill something, death can't kill anymore.

God might have said 'Death, if I can get you to kill something, you can't kill any more. You've got to kill something, I know, because that's my Word. I gave you that power. But, if I can get you to kill me, you can't kill them.'

That's why death has died.

[14] In as much then as the children have partaken of flesh and blood, He Himself likewise shared in the same, that through death He might destroy him who had the power of death, that is, the devil,

[15] and release those who through fear of death were all their lifetime subject to bondage. Hebrews 2:14-15 (NKJV)

[7]"The Law of God demanded and does demand death for sin. The soul that sinneth, it shall die. The wages of sin is death. Satan was the cause of man's sin in the first place and, even though he is a usurper, he can claim, justly so in a sense, that the sinner must die. He had the power, the authority to demand that every sinner should pay sin's penalty. And on account of this all men, because all are sinners, were fearful of death and subject to bondage, because of sin, to serve it and thus serve Satan."   E. Schuyler English

Chapter Six

The Court Room

Death reigned from Adam to Moses, even over those who had not sinned. When Adam sinned, death came upon all men and women. Now, we have many fields partially filled with dead people.

Because of God's Word you and I will have to die physically and go to the grave. Just as a judge in a courtroom holds court, considers and evaluates the evidence of a pending case, he now must pass judgment on the defendant. If the defendant is found guilty, a sentence is handed down by the judge in that black robe and will be carried out as designed. If not guilty the defended is set free.

In the courtroom of spiritual law and justice a judgment of exonerated will be handed down to all those who have accepted the death of Christ in their stead. This exoneration occurs when a person who has been convicted of a crime is later proved to have been innocent of that crime.

³⁰ since there is one God who will justify the circumcised by faith and the uncircumcised through faith. Romans 3:30 (NKJV)

Now, when God told Adam the day you eat you will surely die, God was giving rights to death. In other words he was saying to death if Adam disobeys me, you have a right to kill him. Death can judge and that's why death can kill every sinner.

Sin gives death the right to kill. Therefore, the only way to avoid death is to get rid of sin in your life. The question becomes what can you do with sin to get rid of death?

Death can only be justified by death. God promised Satan a death that would solve the problem.

¹⁴ So the Lord God said to the serpent: "Because you have done this, you *are* cursed more than all cattle, and more than every beast of the field; on your

belly you shall go, and you shall eat dust all the days of your life.

[15] And I will put enmity between you and the woman, and between your seed and her Seed; He shall bruise your head, and you shall bruise His heel." Genesis 3:14-15

In other words the woman shall have a seed and this seed shall be at enmity with you Satan, and He will crush your head and you will bruise His heel.

God talking to Satan says, 'He will crush your head. You will bruise his heel.' In other words when Satan bruises Him, Jesus is going crush Satan.

When he put His death down, His death will destroy Satan's power."

An interesting relationship between death and power is found in Romans 6:8-11.

[8] Now if we have died with Christ, we believe that we shall also live with Him,

[9] Because we know that Christ (the Anointed One), being once raised from the dead, will never die again; death no longer has power over Him.

[10] For by the death He died, He died to sin [ending His relation to it] once for

all; and the life that He lives, He is living to God [in unbroken fellowship with Him]

[11] Even so consider yourselves also dead to sin and your relation to it broken, but alive to God [living in unbroken fellowship with Him] in Christ Jesus.   Romans 6:8-11 (AMP)

Therefore, because Christ defeated death when He rose again, death lost its power.

Also in Hebrews we see:

[8] You have put all things in subjection under his feet. For in that He put all in subjection under him, He left nothing that is not put under him. But now we do not yet see all things put under him.

[9] But we see Jesus, who was made a little lower than the angels, for the suffering of death crowned with glory and honor, that He, by the grace of God, might taste death for everyone. Hebrews 2:8-9 (NKJV)

He chose to taste death for every one which includes all 6.2 billion people on earth today. Not one of them has to go to hell.

Jesus was made a sacrificial offering, in order to bring many sons and daughters to glory. So this suffering death by Jesus established a state of exoneration for the sinner, who would simply accept His death by faith and be set free as if they had never been guilty of missing the mark.

My conclusion of the whole matter is in I Corinthians, chapter fifteen.

> [56.] The sting of death is sin, and the strength of sin is the law.

> [57.] But thanks be to God, who gives us the victory through our Lord Jesus Christ.

> [58.] Therefore, my beloved brethren, be steadfast, immovable, always abounding in the work of the Lord, knowing that your labor is not in vain in the Lord.
> 1 Corinthians 15:56-58 (NKJV)

God's solution to death was the promise of a seed that would destroy the power of death.

What is the power of death? According to the word of God, the power of death is sin! And the source of sin is rebellion which is found in the heart of Satan.

The Bible says that Christ came to destroy him who had the power of death. And it is Satan that had it. He gave man the spirit of rebellion as well and man also obtained the power of death. Therefore, man became a victim of death, because of the sin he committed due to his disobedience of God's word.

Chapter Seven

Choose Life

It is said that cigarette smoking may be harmful to your health and if that is the case my dear friend, whom I met on a bus trip, was beginning to contaminate and befoul his body, not knowing that his body belongs to the Lord. The life that he wants and so much desire are now slowly being smothered by a film of smoke. This smoke could easily result into sickness. We, who are in our right mind, would not defile our own bodies in this way!

Because of the wrong choice and sometimes, a hidden agenda of Satan, there are those who smoke, drink, do drugs, or eat the wrong foods causing sickness in their bodies. I don't believe this is the will of God for our lives. How could it be?

Sickness and disease could not be the will of God for his people.

As a result of sin, death became the ultimate destruction of the physical body. Therefore, if God put sickness, disease and death on us, He would be destroying His own temple.

As a bus driver, I had the opportunity to transport a group of people to West Virginia. While sitting on the bus waiting for the people, I observed a young man smoking a cigarette. In his hand was a book by T.D. Jakes. The book was entitled, Let Him Go. He also had a couple of gold chains around his neck, one with the emblem of *praying hands*. The young man was dressed very modestly in a short walking suit and designer tennis shoes.

As I observed him from a distance, I thought of death at work, especially when he disembarked from the bus. To light up a second cigarette in the few minutes before departing, he was slowly destroying his own body.

After our departure and about fifty minutes into our trip, he approached me with a question. "How much longer do we have to go?" I chuckled within, knowing, he needed a break for another cigarette. I responded politely by saying, "We have approximately one hour and ten minutes, but we'll take a break at the next rest area."

He seemed to be satisfied for the moment. The conversation continued with small talk as to how long I had been driving and how is this bus company compared to others. We then talked a bit about the book he was reading. He shared that he was having a number of questions answered that were in his mind through reading the book.

His experience in growing up was in a home without a father and now his question is, "Why do I do some of the things I do?"

He continued, "After twenty plus years of life, I'm now developing a relationship with my father and some questions are being answered, but not all."

"There is still the struggle of life" he said. I mentioned to him about a fellow in the Bible who had encountered a similar experience, when he would do good, evil was always present. It goes like this:

15. What I don't understand about myself is that I decide one way, but then I act another, doing things I absolutely despise.

16. So if I can't be trusted to figure out what is best for myself and then do it, it becomes obvious that God's command is necessary.

17. But I need something *more*! For if I know the law but still can't keep it, and if the power of sin within me keeps

sabotaging my best intentions, I obviously need help!

18. I realize that I don't have what it takes. I can will it, but I can't *do* it.

19. I decide to do good, but I don't really do it; I decide not to do bad, but then I do it anyway.

20. My decisions, such as they are, don't result in actions. Something has gone wrong deep within me and gets the better of me every time. Romans 7:14-20 (Message Bible)

Of course, I gave the Wilson version, but I concluded that this fellow, the Apostle Paul, found freedom in the same chapter with an explanation of that freedom in the next chapter.

Let's look at it:

His pain and frustration (Rom 7:24)

24. I've tried everything and nothing helps. I'm at the end of my rope. Is there no one who can do anything for me? Isn't that the real question?

His answer, God's plan, sanctification (Romans 7:25)

> [25.] The answer, thank God, is that Jesus Christ can and does. He acted to set things right in this life of contradictions where I want to serve God with all my heart and mind, but I am pulled by the influence of sin to do something totally different. Romans 7:24-25 Message Bible

His explanation, a new position, in Christ (Romans 8:1-5)

> [1] There is therefore now no condemnation to them which are in Christ Jesus, who walk not after the flesh, but after the Spirit.

> [2] For the law of the Spirit of life in Christ Jesus hath made me free from the law of sin and death."

> [3] For what the law could not do, in that it was weak through the flesh, God sending his own Son in the likeness of sinful flesh, and for sin, condemned sin in the flesh:

⁴ That the righteousness of the law might be fulfilled in us, who walk not after the flesh, but after the Spirit.

⁵ For they that are after the flesh do mind the things of the flesh; but they that are after the Spirit the things of the Spirit.

I quoted to him the Scripture, "For the law of the Spirit of life in Christ Jesus hath made me free from the law of sin and death." I easily knew that Scripture; that's part of the revelation of this book.

Another version from The Message Bible is as follows:

¹ With the arrival of Jesus, the Messiah, that fateful dilemma is resolved. Those who enter into Christ's being-here-for-us no longer have to live under a continuous, low-lying black cloud.

² A new power is in operation. The Spirit of life in Christ, like a strong wind, has magnificently cleared the air, freeing you from a fated lifetime of brutal tyranny at the hands of sin and death.   Romans 8:1-2(Message Bible)

I followed with a brief explanation, and he said, "Where is that found again? I don't want to forget that."

Our conversation ended when he said, "Here, this is from me." He handed me a generous tip and returned to his seat! I concluded, despite all the challenges, obstacles and outer appearances, God was at work in this man's life!

Life had come to his door and he was recognizing it slowly! This leads us to the question, 'Is life at your door and do you recognize it?' Have you failed to see the potential surrounding you?

Hebrews 2:14 says that Jesus came that he might destroy him that had the power of death! This Scripture is a very powerful Scripture and compacted with infinite details. I will revisit this in chapter nine, but for now, let's look at it in the NKJV:

> [14] Inasmuch then as the children have partaken of flesh and blood, He Himself likewise shared in the same, that through death He might destroy him who had the power of death, that is, the devil. Hebrews 2:14 (NKJV)

Therefore, Jesus was able to render death inoperative, and as a child of God, Satan's power over death is limited in our lives. Satan cannot take us out arbitrarily; he must have our cooperation and/or our words. Negative choices in life have a great deal to do with the amount of access Satan has in our lives.

Notice, the following scriptures will urge us to choose life and why.

[15] "See, I have set before you today life and good, death and evil,

[16] in that I command you today to love the Lord your God, to walk in His ways, and to keep His commandments, His statutes, and His judgments, that you may live and multiply; and the Lord your God will bless you in the land which you go to possess.

[17] But if your heart turns away so that you do not hear, and are drawn away, and worship other gods and serve them,

[18] I announce to you today that you shall surely perish; you shall not prolong your days in the land which you cross over the Jordan to go in and possess.

[19] I call heaven and earth as witnesses today against you, that I have set before you life and death, blessing and

cursing; therefore choose life, that both you and your descendants may live;

20 that you may love the Lord your God, that you may obey His voice, and that you may cling to Him, for He is your life and the length of your days; and that you may dwell in the land which the Lord swore to your fathers, to Abraham, Isaac, and Jacob, to give them." Deuteronomy 30:15-20 (NKJV)

One example of choosing life is seen in the story of the good king, Hezekiah, an outstanding king. There was none like him after David. He did that which was right in the sight of the Lord. However, the prophet Isaiah came to him in 2 Kings and told him he was going die.

1 In those days Hezekiah was sick and near death. And Isaiah the prophet, the son of Amoz, went to him and said to him, "Thus says the Lord: 'Set your house in order, for you shall die, and not live.' "
2 Then he turned his face toward the wall, and prayed to the Lord, saying,
3 "Remember now, O Lord, I pray, how I have walked before You in truth and with a loyal heart, and have done *what was* good in Your sight." And Hezekiah wept bitterly.

> ⁴ And it happened, before Isaiah had gone out into the middle court, that the word of the Lord came to him, saying,
> ⁵ "Return and tell Hezekiah the leader of My people, 'Thus says the Lord, the God of David your father: "I have heard your prayer, I have seen your tears; surely I will heal you. On the third day you shall go up to the house of the Lord.
> ⁶ And I will add to your days fifteen years.
>
> 2 Kings 20:1-6 (NKJV)

Sadly enough, Hezekiah's time to die was at hand. Since this man of God had lived an extraordinary life before God he was neither afraid nor disheartened to present his case before the eternal King of Glory. I don't know totally what Hezekiah was thinking, he may have considered he had no heir to the throne, or there may have been other things he wanted to pursue, maybe he just wanted to live on, or maybe the old colloquial, "I am scared to death!" Whatever the case, God granted his request and added an additional fifteen years to his life and showed him a sign to document that the God of the universe would do exactly what he said.

This is an amazing example of an omniscient, omnipotent God that would hear and not only hear but respond immediately without hesitation to a fleshly dwelling. We should think it not strange for the God whom we serve to answer our prayer even when He knows the outcome may be that of dismay. How immense the grief that resulted!

In 2 Chronicles 32:25, the story continues:

> [25] But Hezekiah did not repay according to the favor *shown* him, for his heart was lifted up; therefore wrath was looming over him and over Judah and Jerusalem. [26] Then Hezekiah humbled himself for the pride of his heart, he and the inhabitants of Jerusalem, so that the wrath of the Lord did not come upon them in the days of Hezekiah.
>
> 2 Chronicles 32:25-26 (NKJV)

Sons were born and the one son, Manasseh, succeeded his father to the throne. Manasseh was twelve years old when he began his reign, a reign of disgrace and ruthlessness and ruled not a few years but for fifty-five. A son who was the worst king that ever reigned in the southern kingdom. He worshiped the sun, moon, and stars, and all the hosts of heaven. He established idol worship, caused his son to pass through the fire (or sacrificed to idols), practiced soothsaying, used witchcraft, and consulted spiritualists and mediums. He did much evil in the sight of the Lord. He set a carved image called Asherah. He dismantled everything that his father had done. According to Jewish tradition he had his father's best friend, Isaiah, sawed in half.

The moral of this story or the conclusion of the whole matter is even though we may live an extended period of time the extension is pointless unless we serve God, keep His commandments, meet God's conditions for salvation, reverence, worship, and obey Him.

In Roman 10:9 we are given the formula for salvation which in turn is life.

> [9] That if thou shalt confess with thy mouth the Lord Jesus, and shalt believe in thine heart that God hath raised Him from the dead, thou shalt be saved.

> [10] For with the heart man believeth unto righteousness; and with the mouth confession is made unto salvation.

We can choose life by simply being obedient to God's Word. Look at the choice from Proverbs 18:21. It confirms that we have a choice between life and death.

> [21] Death and life *are* in the power of the tongue, and those who love it will eat its fruit. Proverbs 18:21 (NKJV)

Death is not only an enemy to us, but also an enemy to Christ. At the end, death too shall die.

> [24] Then comes the end, when He delivers the kingdom to God the Father, when He puts an end to all rule and all authority and power.

> [25] For He must reign till He has put all enemies under His feet.

> [26] The last enemy that will be destroyed is death.

> [27] For "He has put all things under His feet." But when He says "all things are put under Him," it is evident that He who put all things under Him is accepted. 1 Corinthians 15:24-27 (NKJV)

Paul gives us the view that life and death are ours to choose.

> [21] Therefore let no one boast in men. For all things are yours:

> [22] whether Paul or Apollos or Cephas, or the world or life or death, or things

present or things to come--all are yours.
1 Corinthians 3:21-22 (NKJV)

Look at the choice that the Apostle Paul
makes in the book of Philippians, and the reason he
makes it.

[20] according to my earnest expectation
and hope that in nothing I shall be
ashamed, but with all boldness, as
always, so now also Christ will be
magnified in my body, whether by life
or by death.

[21] For to me, to live is Christ, and to die
is gain.

[22] But if I live on in the flesh, this will
mean fruit from my labor; yet what I
shall choose I cannot tell.

[23] For I am hard pressed between the
two, having a desire to depart and be
with Christ, which is far better.

[24] Nevertheless, to remain in the flesh is
more needful for you.

[25] And being confident of this, I know
that I shall remain and continue with

you all for your progress and joy of faith. Philippians 1:20-25 (NKJV)

The Message Bible says it like this:

[20.] I can hardly wait to continue on my course. I don't expect to be embarrassed in the least. On the contrary, everything happening to me in this jail only serves to make Christ more accurately known, regardless of whether I live or die. They didn't shut me up; they gave me a pulpit!

[21] Alive, I'm Christ's messenger; dead, I'm his bounty. Life versus even more life! I can't lose.

[22] As long as I'm alive in this body, there is good work for me to do. If I had to choose right now, I hardly know which I'd choose.

[23] Hard choice! The desire to break camp here and be with Christ is powerful. Some days I can think of nothing better.

[24] But most days, because of what you

are going through, I am sure that it's better for me to stick it out here.

^{25} So I plan to be around awhile, companion to you as your growth and joy in this life of trusting God continues. Philippians 1:20-25 (MSG)

He has to make a choice and it's a hard choice. His conclusion is to stay around for a while.

We learn from history that Paul was beheaded. History also tells us that he made a choice to go to Jerusalem, knowing that he would be bound and subject to death. Let's look at Acts 21.

^{10} And as we stayed many days, a certain prophet named Agabus came down from Judea.

^{11} When he had come to us, he took Paul's belt, bound his *own* hands and feet, and said, "Thus says the Holy Spirit, 'So shall the Jews at Jerusalem bind the man who owns this belt, and deliver *him* into the hands of the Gentiles.' "

^{12} Now when we heard these things, both we and those from that place pleaded with him not to go up to Jerusalem.

[13]Then Paul answered, What mean ye to weep and to break mine heart? for I am ready not to be bound only, but also to die at Jerusalem for the name of the Lord Jesus.

[14] And when he would not be persuaded, we ceased, saying, the will of the Lord be done.   Acts 21:10-14 (NKJV)

Knowing the consequences of his journey to Jerusalem, Paul chose to make the trip. This was a trip that   would eventually lead to his physical death. Yet he was ready to not only be bound, but to die at Jerusalem for the name of the Lord Jesus. While at Jerusalem, at the feast of Pentecost, he was almost murdered by a Jewish mob in the temple. Rescued from their violence by the Roman commander, he was conveyed as a prisoner to Caesarea, where, due to various causes, he was detained as a prisoner for two years in Herod's praetorium (Acts 23:35).

This first imprisonment came at to a close, with Paul being acquitted, probably because no witnesses appeared against him. Once more he set out on his missionary labors, visiting Western and Eastern Europe and Asia Minor. During this period of freedom, he wrote his first epistle to Timothy and his epistle to Titus. The year of his release was highlighted by the burning of Rome, which Nero saw fit to attribute to the Christians.

A fierce persecution now broke out against the Christians. Paul was seized, and once more sent to Rome as a prisoner.

During this imprisonment, he probably wrote his second epistle to Timothy, the last he ever wrote. There can be little doubt that he appeared again at Nero's bar, and this time the charge did not break down.

Easton's Illustrated Dictionary says, [8]"In all history there is not a more startling illustration of the irony of human life than this scene of Paul at the bar of Nero. On the judgment-seat, clad in the imperial purple, sat a man who, in a bad world, had attained the eminence of being the very worst and meanest being in it. A man stained with every crime. A man whose whole being was so steeped in every nameable and unnamable vice, that the body and soul of him were, as some one said at the time, nothing but a compound of mud and blood. In the prisoner's dock stood the best man the world possessed, his hair whitened with labors for the good of men and the glory of God."

"The trial ended. Paul was condemned and delivered over to the executioner. He was led out of the city with a crowd of the lowest rabble at his heels. The fatal spot was reached; he knelt beside the block; the headsman's axe gleamed in the sun and fell; and the head of the greatest apostle of the world rolled down in the dust."

This was (probably A.D. 66), four years before the fall of Jerusalem. Did he pray to be released from prison? There is no record to show that he inquired of the Lord concerning his freedom.

However, he did pray in Acts 16:25 and was set free via earthquake. When Peter was imprisoned, God sent an angel to let him out (Acts 12:5-11). The prayers of the Church produced a miraculous interference without which Peter may not have escaped. But there was prayer. Why did Paul not pray? Why did the Lord not come to the rescue of Paul as he had done before?

[25] But at midnight Paul and Silas were praying and singing hymns to God, and the prisoners were listening to them.

[26] Suddenly there was a great earthquake, so that the foundations of the prison were shaken; and immediately all the doors were opened and everyone's chains were loosed.

Acts 16:25-26 (NKJV)

Perhaps the answers to the above questions are found in his letter to Timothy where Paul was ready to die and be in the presence of the Lord.

[6] For I am already being poured out as a drink offering, and the time of my departure is at hand.

[7] I have fought the good fight, I have finished the race, I have kept the faith.

[8] Finally, there is laid up for me the crown of righteousness, which the Lord, the righteous Judge, will give to me on that Day, and not to me only but also to all who have loved His appearing.   2 Timothy 4:6-8 (NKJV)

The Message Bible says it like this:

[6] You take over. I'm about to die, my life an offering on God's altar.

[7] This is the only race worth running. I've run hard right to the finish, believed all the way.

[8] All that's left now is the shouting— God's applause! 2 Timothy 4:6-8 (MSG)

Chapter Eight

A Satisfied Life

In the middle of life is that great word "if". This "if" is predicated upon a positive decision if one is to live (abundant) life. Of course, we live by choosing life through Jesus Christ. The greatest decision one can make is to follow Jesus and if we follow Jesus, He has promised many blessings, coupled with a long and satisfying life.

Let's look at Psalm 91.

> [16] With long life I will satisfy him, and show him My salvation." Psalms 91:16 (NKJV)

At the very end of Psalm 91, the Spirit of the Lord leaves no room for doubting that the Father God is prepared to bless His children with a long and satisfying life. But, this life is foundational upon the laws of God. You are not likely to live such a life in the absence of keeping the commandments and pleasing God. Again we have the big "if". We must keep His commands and please God. If not, we suffer the consequences.

> [22] And whatever we ask we receive from Him, because we keep His commandments and do those things that are pleasing in His sight. 1 John 3:22 (NKJV)

When your life is pleasing to God, you can expect Him to hear and answer your prayer. Many things in life are the way they are simply, because we expect them to be that way. We think it, we talk it, and we prepare for it to be that way. We must stop speaking and preparing for a rainy day or we are going to have some rain.

My brother once asked me, "Don't heart problems run in our family?" I responded, "If they do, it stopped when it got to me."

How often have you heard someone say, "Such and such a disease runs in my family?" Years later, that person is admitted to the hospital for treatment for that very same disease.

Unless we change our way of thinking to conform to what the Word of God says about life, we will always be subject to what others say about sickness and disease, death and dying.

In our country, we commonly hold to the age of 65 as the age of retirement and following that the 'golden years.' What are the 'golden years?' Some call it living life at ease; others just say a good life.

Do we wait till age 65 to begin to have a good life? Is this the destiny that God has chosen for us? I think not! Joshua was 80 years old when he crossed the Jordan River into the land of Canaan and his next conquest was the city of Jericho.

But, when a person reaches 65, the assumption is made that he or she really cannot work as well as before. This age is completely arbitrary. It has nothing to do with the person's own ability, skills, or physical and mental health. They are just encouraged, sometimes even pressured, to leave the work force simply because they have reached the age of 65.

If we are not careful, what happens is that all our life we will think about retiring at age 65. (This is the age the author is approaching slowly.) Speaking and thinking this way will likely to do something to us if we are not careful. It could slow us down. It could slow down our productivity as we are approaching this age.

What happens next? We will stay at home, and what will we end up doing? Chances are, not much of anything, because we have conditioned ourselves to believe that we are now at the age where we cannot do a whole lot.

Another expectation that comes with age is that aches and pains are part of getting older. So now, rather than stand up to any foul symptom that tries to attack our body, as we would have when we were younger, we automatically accept it. One will usually say, "Well, this ache and pain goes with my age. This is just part of the territory". That's the word that is most frequently heard and prone to be accepted.

If we submit to this way of thinking, this is precisely how we will end up, even though God says He wants us to be satisfied with a long life. In case you didn't know, being old and decrepit hardly equates with being satisfied with a long life. The general public's idea about living long is certainly not God's best and is not the way it has to be. Yet, it will be this way for us if we expect it, because we have believed the general public's popular opinion.

Therefore, we need to stop expecting what people say and start expecting what the Word of God says. This means we will have to change our way of thinking. We will have to stop saying I'm saving for a rainy day and begin expecting sunshine all the way through.

That is not to say we are not to save money, neither is it to say that there will not be any rain nor pain, but we should expect and confess God's word over our lives. Look for the long and satisfying life, expecting a body that is healed and whole and well. We must renew our minds to think about us the way God thinks about us.

We must refuse to let age limit us. When God spoke to Moses, He said, "I am the God of thy father, the God of Abraham, the God of Isaac, and the God of Jacob." (Exodus 3:6).

As Superman in the comics and TV superstar had super power and was always on the spot with incredible timing, Abraham had Superman faith. He wasn't afraid to follow after God, even if it bucked popular opinion. Abraham was about seventy-five years old and trying to retire when God told him to get up and get out of town.

> [1] Now the Lord had said to Abram: "Get out of your country, from your family and from your father's house, to a land that I will show you.
>
> [2] I will make you a great nation; I will bless you and make your name great; and you shall be a blessing.
>
> Genesis 12:1-2 (NKJV)

Abraham heard the voice of God and his Superman faith went into action. He didn't mind breaking tradition or bucking popular opinion to follow after the voice of God. But, it was a strange thing God asked him to do ... and what came next was even stranger!

God said, "And I will make of thee a great nation, and I will bless thee, and make thy name great; and thou shalt be a blessing: And I will bless them that bless thee, and curse him that curseth thee: and in thee shall all families of the earth be blessed."(Genesis 12:2-3).

Now, you've got to understand something: Abraham was seventy-five years young. If he wanted to get somewhere, he had to walk, ride a camel or a donkey. I don't think he had a Rolls Royce. Can you imagine Abe's initial reaction to this idea?

But whatever his thoughts or ideas, Abraham didn't argue with God. He had an attitude that spoke volumes. An attitude that said, "If God said it I'll do it." Superman faith in a human is adventurous! Few men have lived a more adventurous life in their golden years than Abraham! The man went against the flow. His life was about following God when he knew not where God was leading. His leaving home for an unknown land resulted in becoming rich, healthy and happy. With that he became the father of many nations.

God cut a covenant with him and told him many things. There were times he saw angels and the future too. Abraham didn't live a dull life! It was long and satisfying life. It was his faith in God that brought him such an incredible life. He just believed and trusted in God.

God called things that were not as though they were and they came into existence. Abraham did too. Abraham kept it simple: Follow God, believe God and, if you mess up, ask for forgiveness and learn from the mistake! He may not have done everything right, but his heart was right and he showed us what it meant to walk by Superman faith.

The Bible says in Chapter 28 of Deuteronomy that they (God's people) were subject to the curse of the law, if they were not obeying God.

> [15] "But it shall come to pass, if you do not obey the voice of the Lord your God, to observe carefully all His commandments and His statutes which I command you today, that all these curses will come upon you and overtake you: Deuteronomy 28:15 (NKJV)

And this disobedience would bring a curse that would shorten their expected life span. Notice the "if". (Just a side liner here: it would be better to be cussed out than to be cursed out. There is a difference, you know). On the other hand, if they were obedient to God's word the following are the results. Again notice the 'if.'

[1] "Now it shall come to pass, if you diligently obey the voice of the Lord your God, to observe carefully all His commandments which I command you today, that the Lord your God will set you high above all nations of the earth. Deuteronomy 28:1 (NKJV)

Christians, however, are not bound by this curse!

[13] Christ has redeemed us from the curse of the law, having become a curse for us (for it is written, *"Cursed is everyone who hangs on a tree"*). Gal. 3:13 (NKJV)

In Psalms 91:14-16, David says "With long life will I satisfy him". So, we are to live until we are satisfied. Before we get ready to go home to be with the Lord, we should be satisfied and we should choose to go.

The prerequisite to qualifying for this long life is at the beginning of this Psalm. "He that dwelleth in the secret place of the Most High shall abide under the shadow of the Almighty." The word dwell means to live in, settle down in, and take up residence in. This means live by the Word of God!

It is when we are under the shadow of the Almighty that we have protection from the devastating effects of sin, and the net result will be just what the psalmist says, a long and satisfied life.

Chapter Nine

Life through the Blood

In the beginning, God did something profound. The first thing God did for man was to bless him.

> ^{22} And God blessed them, saying, "Be fruitful and multiply, and fill the waters in the seas, and let birds multiply on the earth."   Genesis 1:22 (NKJV)

With the fall of man, one of the things mankind lost was the original blessing of God. That's why Adam was told he would have to work by the sweat of his brow from then on.

Any blessings that were given in the Bible up until Jesus' death on the cross were given at God's discretion. When He found a man who He deemed righteous, like Abraham, God blessed him.

When Jesus came and shed His blood for all of humanity, He did it to bridge the gap between God and man, to set things right once again. One of the things Jesus' blood and death did was to break the curse of sin and get back the original blessing. All the curses that came upon mankind because of the fall, were hung on Jesus when He was crucified.

Through the sacrifice of Jesus for all of humanity, He opened the door for you and me to receive the full blessings of God once again. Jesus broke the power of man's original sin - and the curses that came afterwards! That's why Christians can say that, through Jesus, the curse has been broken over their lives, and that through His blood they are blessed. It is through the blood that we're entitled to the blessings of Abraham.

On the cross, Jesus broke the power of sin! Jesus broke the power of hell, death, and the grave! Jesus broke the power of sickness, disease, and poverty! All the curses of sin were broken through the blood that was shed by Jesus on Calvary.

Now, let's look at how he did it. The Father God, from the beginning, being omnipotent, all powerful, created man. You knew that. But the unique way he did it, is not known to everyone.

27 So God created man in His *own* image; in the image of God He created him; male and female He created them. Genesis 1:27 (NKJV)

21 And the Lord God caused a deep sleep to fall on Adam, and he slept; and He took one of his ribs, and closed up the flesh in its place.

22 Then the rib which the Lord God had taken from man He made into a woman, and He brought her to the man. Genesis 2:21-22 (NKJV)

Now let's revisit the Scripture in Hebrews the second chapter.

14 Inasmuch then as the children have partaken of flesh and blood, He Himself likewise shared in the same, that through death He might destroy him who had the power of death, that is, the devil. Hebrews 2:14 (NKJV)

I like the KJV just a little better especially the words 'took part' which will better serve our purpose.

¹⁴ Forasmuch then as the children are partakers of flesh and blood, he also himself likewise took part of the same; that through death he might destroy him that had the power of death, that is, the devil;

Hebrews 2:14 (KJV)

This scripture is most interesting and shows God's concern for man's mortality. God, from the beginning, shows Himself to be Jehovah-Jireh: the Lord our Provider, Gen. 22:14. This is the God who foresees our sinful state and, <u>in advance,</u> provides for it.

From the Greek the original word translated "partaker", means share fully. This means all of Adams descendents share fully in his flesh and blood. The sinfulness of the first Adam is the sinfulness departed to his children. In other words, this sin germ descended through the Adamic posterity, making us all sinners from birth. This means the children sharing fully. Another way of saying it is all of mankind is born in a sinful state and has a need to be born again.

When we read 'He also himself likewise took part,' we must recognize from the Greek, the original word translated "part", means that he only took part, <u>not all</u>. When we understand that Jesus took part, He took some part, not all. The children share fully in the flesh and blood, but Jesus shared only in the flesh.

[9]"According to the flesh, He was the seed of Adam, but the blood in the veins of Jesus came by way of the supernatural conception of the Holy Spirit. If Jesus had been born in the human way in which children are conceived today, He would have been as sinful as any other child that is born of the seed of Adam and share fully in Adams' flesh and blood."

"But since life is in the blood and not in the flesh, Jesus could have a body born of the flesh of Mary and still have no sin, if He had not the blood of Adam. The blood in the veins of Jesus came to him by way of the conception of the Holy Spirit."

Life is in the blood.

[14] For *it is* the life of all flesh; the blood of it *is* for the life thereof: therefore I said unto the children of Israel, Ye shall eat the blood of no manner of flesh: for the life of all flesh *is* the blood thereof: whosoever eateth it shall be cut off. Leviticus 17:14 (KJV)

[9]"This proves conclusively that sin is transmitted through the blood and not through the flesh. Science definitely recognizes that the blood which flows in an unborn baby's arteries and veins is not derived from the mother, but is produced only

after the introduction of the male sperm. There is not one drop of the mother's blood that ever enters into the unborn child's arteries and veins. The blood is produced within the embryo itself but only after the egg has been fertilized by the sperm."

The mother provides the unborn developing infant with all the nutrients necessary for the building of the baby's body, but all the blood that is formed is formed in the embryo itself and only as a result of the contribution of the male parent.

From the time of conception to the time of the birth of the infant, not one single drop of blood ever passes from the mother to the child.

[10]"The placenta forming union between mother and child is so constructed that all the nutrients such as protein, fat, carbohydrates, salts, minerals, and antibiotics pass freely from mother to child and the waste products of the child's metabolism is passed back to the mother's circulation. There occurs, normally, no interchange of a single drop of blood. All the blood which is in the child is produced within the child itself as results of the introduction by the male sperm. The mother contributes no blood to the child."

How wonderful that God, foreseeing our need from the beginning, prepared the virgin birth of His son Jesus. When He created woman, He created her so that her blood would not pass from her to the offspring. The blood is a result of the male and not the female.

God, in order to produce a sinless man who was also the son of Adam, or a descendent of, had to provide a way for a human body to be derived from Adam and yet not have one single drop of Adam's blood in his vein.

This is the scientific biological reason for the sinlessness of the Son of Man, Christ Jesus. Jesus was sinless because He was conceived by the Holy Spirit with no sin in him. Yet was born of the Virgin Mary and had a body of flesh like yours and mine.

[9]"Conception by the Holy Spirit was the only way the virgin birth could be accomplished. Mary contributed to the body of Jesus and He became the seed of David according to the flesh. The Holy Ghost contributed to the blood of Jesus. Therefore, in His arteries and veins there was sinless blood. It was divine blood. It was precious blood and there has never been any like it and nor will there be any like it in the future. That is why Judas confessed in Matthew 27 saying he had betrayed the innocent blood."

[3] Then Judas, His betrayer, seeing that He had been condemned, was remorseful and brought back the thirty pieces of silver to the chief priests and elders

[4] saying, "I have sinned by betraying innocent blood." And they said, "What

is that to us? You see to it!" Matthew
27:3-4 (NKJV)

Human blood is corruptible, but Christ's
blood is incorruptible. Divine conception is
incorruptible. Sin made the original human blood
corruptible. The original sin of Adam and Eve was
'blood poisoning' and since we are partakers of the
flesh and blood of Adam and Eve, our blood is
contaminated to the extend that there is no hope
without a savior who has sinless blood to atone for
our sins.

But thank God, Christ Jesus with the sinless
blood died for our sins, purchased our salvation and
shed his blood for the atoning of our sins. This is all,
so that we might be made free.

> [18] And having been set free from sin,
> you became slaves of righteousness.
> Romans 6:18 (NKJV)

> [1] *There is* therefore now no
> condemnation to those who are in
> Christ Jesus, who do not walk
> according to the flesh, but according to
> the Spirit.

> [2] For the law of the Spirit of life in
> Christ Jesus has made me free from the

law of sin and death. Romans 8:1-2 (NKJV)

[6] "And when I passed by you and saw you struggling in your own blood, I said to you in your blood, 'Live!' Yes, I said to you in your blood, 'Live!' Ezekiel 16:6 (NKJV)

Jesus Christ said something very interesting.

"Whoso eateth my flesh, and drinketh my blood, hath eternal life; and I will raise him up at the last day. For my flesh is meat indeed, and my blood is drink indeed. He that eateth my flesh, and drinketh my blood, dwelleth in me, and I in him." John 6:54-56

Because the life of the flesh is in the blood, Jesus is saying that we are to accept His shed blood for our sins by faith and then we receive life. Jesus shed His blood and gave His life. The life is in the blood.
This is why the innocent blood of Jesus could atone for the sins of mankind and give us life through the blood, making us immediately free upon the acceptance of Jesus Christ.

[6] 'And then I came by. I saw you all miserable and bloody. Yes, I said to you, lying there helpless and filthy, Live!'
Ezekiel 16:6 (MSG)

Chapter Ten

The Thief of Life

J esus said: "The thief comes to steal, to kill, and to destroy: I am come that they might have life, and that they might have it more abundantly." (John 10:10)

Satan Is the Thief of Life. Our inheritance in God's Word promises us at least threescore years and ten; and if by reason of strength they be fourscore years, there is till labor and sorrow. But, because Satan is such a thief, he will still try to take your life before you are seventy years of age.

> [10] The days of our lives *are* seventy years; and if by reason of strength *they*

are eighty years, yet their boast *is* only labor and sorrow; For it is soon cut off, and we fly away.   Psalms 90:10 (NKJV)

If you want to receive your full inheritance of a long and satisfying life, you have to study everything and do all you know to do spiritually, physically, and mentally. It is not enough to just say "The will of the Lord be done." The will of the Lord is for you to know and do His Word (His will). You cannot put off on God what He has given you the responsibility of doing.

Hosea gives us a unique view of a life shorter than normal. As a matter of fact, he speaks of destruction in life.

[6] My people are destroyed for lack of knowledge. Because you have rejected knowledge, I also will reject you from being priest for Me; because you have forgotten the law of your God, I also will forget your children.   Hosea 4:6 (NKJV)

In this case, ignorance is not bliss. There were certain spiritual and natural laws God set in place at the foundation of the world. You have to know what these laws are, because, if you violate any of them, whether knowingly or unknowingly, there is a price that you will have to pay.

Any judge will tell you that ignorance of the law, simply not knowing the law, is no excuse. You are still liable for having broken the law and you are going to have to pay one way or another. The enemy will be there to bring an accusation.

> [10] Then I heard a loud voice saying in heaven, "Now salvation, and strength, and the kingdom of our God, and the power of His Christ have come, for the accuser of our brethren, who accused them before our God day and night, has been cast down. Revelation 12:10 (NKJV)

You see he is the accuser of the brethren.

Be not fretful when you see others appearing to prosper with long life, although they are frequently engaged in habits that the doctor says will kill you.

I know of a long time schoolmate, who drinks almost daily, yet he lives. Another school mate of mine accepted Christ and was dead a few years later. The latter schoolmate was a threat to the kingdom of Satan and was taken out through deception.

It would appear that the devil is not after anyone who is not a threat to his dominion on the earth (These people are usually his anyway.) He will let just enough of these types of people live long lives, so the majority of people will be fooled into thinking that it doesn't matter how you live.

Make no mistake! Satan will come after you, because you became a threat to him when you confessed Jesus Christ as your personal Savior and Lord. Satan will be on your case all the time, waiting for you to open a door to allow him into your life. You must always be alert to his schemes.

Paul speaks of having a choice of living or dying.

> [21] For to me, to live *is* Christ, and to die *is* gain.

> [22] But if *I* live on in the flesh, this *will mean* fruit from *my* labor; yet what I shall choose I cannot tell..

> [23] For I am hard pressed between the two, having a desire to depart and be with Christ, *which is* far better.

> [24] Nevertheless, to remain in the flesh *is* more needful for you.
>
> Philippians 1:21-24 (NKJV)

Death is not to be feared. Death is a great loss to a carnal, worldly man, for he loses all his earthly comforts and all his hopes. But to a true believer it is gain, for it is the end of all his weakness and misery. It delivers him from all the evils of life, and brings him to possess the chief good.

[11]"The apostle's difficulty was not between living in this world and living in heaven; between these two there is no comparison; but between serving Christ in this world and enjoying him in another."

Death, in and of itself, is not something for the Christian to fear. Your flesh or physical body is just the house you live in. When Paul says "I", he is talking about the real him. The point Paul is making is that his fleshly body is just what he is living in at the moment, and he has a say about his flesh, the house he is living in. Paul has a choice as to whether or not he wants to remain living in his body.

Notice also that Paul did not just say, "If I live." No, he qualified this. Paul said "If I live on". You see, Paul was faced not with a choice as to whether he is going to continue living, but whether he wanted to continue living in his flesh-and-blood body. This lets you know that when you physically die, your flesh-and-blood body dies, but the real you, your spirit man, is going to continue living.

So, death can be a gain if you have accepted Jesus Christ.

> [9] That if you confess with your mouth
> the Lord Jesus and believe in your heart
> that God has raised Him from the dead,
> you will be saved.

Romans 10:9 (NKJV)

As a Christian, this life that you are going to continue living must somehow be better, for Paul goes on to add in verse twenty-three, "Having a desire to depart and be with Christ, which is far better".

Yet, there are many people who fear death. In fact, they are being robbed of life because of their fear of dying. I know from personal experience that if you are thinking about death every day, this is a burden that can keep you from doing what you really desire and from living life to its fullest.

Have you ever wanted to go on a cruise but thought it was too much water to drink? Has fear gripped you and paralyzed you? I know some people who will not fly. They are afraid the plane will not reach its destinations safely and if they were on the flight, they would die.

I once encountered the same fear and would not fly, thinking the plane might be hijacked and I would end up being a hostage in another country. Well, after a short encounter with a man of God, all fear dissipated.

The story is this. I desired to take a missionary trip, but was afraid. My mother's pastor, The Late Rev. Willie Brooks, informed me that he had been hospitalized from a car accident and was told by the doctors that he would not live. He then said the Lord spoke to him with these life changing words: "You cannot die till I say so."

He then asked me this astounding question: "Do you mean the Lord has opened a door and you're going to close it?" After pondering these words, I recognized that my life was in the hands of God and that it was God that would care for me and protect me. It would also be Jesus Christ that wanted me to experience an abundance of life and not just a sprinkling.

Once I found out that God is about giving abundant life and saving lives, not taking them, my entire life changed. I was free to see that it makes absolutely no sense to be terrified of death.

My bondage to a fear of death, the thief of life, was broken. I am free to experience all life has to offer me. My objective is to give the thief no place by way of actions or words. For I recognize that the power of life and death is in the tongue.

> [21] Death and life *are* in the power of the tongue, and those who love it will eat its fruit. Proverbs 18:21 (NKJV)

Jesus said in Matthew 7:14 that "Narrow is the gate and difficult is the way which leads to life, and there are few who find it." Since the gate is narrow, you cannot afford to take any unnecessary risks. You need to stick with what the Bible says.

Don't wait until you are under attack by some disease or some symptoms have crept up on you. Start now to ward off anything and everything that the enemy would try to send your way by speaking life, God's Word, to your body.

> [11] And this is the testimony: that God has given us eternal life, and this life is in His Son.
>
> [12] He who has the Son has life; he who does not have the Son of God does not have life.
>
> [13] These things I have written to you who believe in the name of the Son of God, that you may know that you have eternal life, and that you may continue to believe in the name of the Son of God. 1 John 5:11-13 (NKJV)

Does being a Christian mean I have to give up my life (I mean die physically)? Is it possible that Christians are supposed to live their lives for the Lord and not die for the Lord? After all, He died for us, so that we may have life and have it more abundantly.

What better way is there to prove that the Gospel is the Good News and that it is real by being a victorious overcoming <u>living</u> Christian? On the contrary, I am not denying that there have been those who have given their life as a martyr, but in the absence of that, let's LIVE abundantly for the Lord!

Now, if someone you know dies before they have reached at least 70 years of age, do we say that God took them? Does God kill people? Does God take life?

If a Christian dies early, it does not mean that they did not love the Lord or that they will not go to be with the Lord. It just means that they will miss out on years they should have had here, working together with Christ to impact eternity.

Make no mistake. I believe the Lord wants you to receive your full inheritance of what He has promised you in His Word. But just like any other last will and testament, you have to do what it takes to claim this inheritance. You cannot benefit from what Jesus has done for you until you first accept and confess Jesus Christ as your personal Savior and Lord and then do what His Word says. Then, and only then, will Satan no longer have the ability to lord over you through death.

Notice in John 10:10 that Jesus said, "I have come that they may have life". You may, not would!

This means that the abundant life in Christ Jesus is not automatic. You have a part to play in whether you have life and whether you have it more abundantly. The choice is yours!

We should believe God for the very highest level that can possibly be attained in this life. As a believer in the Lord Jesus Christ, obtaining the very best God has for us, (and not allowing the thief to steal from us), to fear God, and keep his commandments, is the whole of man. We just need to bring our expectations and way of thinking into line with what the Bible has to say, and fight all the symptoms, sickness, or disease that will try to come upon us.

"For I know the plans I have for you," declares the Lord, "plans to prosper you and not to harm you, plans to give you hope and a future." (Jeremiah 29:11 NIV) This may be difficult to believe, especially if we have indulged greatly in sin. God can restore what the devil tried to kill, steal and destroy in our lives and allow us to have, in the absence of the thief of life, a real experience of the abundance of life.

Chapter Eleven

Appointment
with Death

It's simple, but not always acknowledged or communicated verbally. Death is really quite simple. Death is the natural sequence of events for man. For the unsaved man, there is judgment after death. If the death of Christ is not accepted as atonement for sin, then there is nothing ahead for them but judgment.

It is appointed unto men once to die or be changed in a moment, in the twinkling of an eye.

> [27] And as it is appointed for men to die once, but after this the judgment.
> Hebrews 9:27 (NKJV)

Notice that 'death' is not appointed unto all men, but there is "appointed unto men once to die." Some are not going to die.

The big question would be can we make the appointment? You probably know or heard of someone who has committed suicide. The question in this abnormal death would be to ask who made the decision.

We often think of not having any control over death but I encourage you to think again. Is it not possible for you to pick up a gun, place it to your head and pull the trigger? Do you have the power to purchase a portion of poisoning, sit down at the table and ingest it, causing death? Of course you would say yes and you're not apt to do either. However, either decision by the one involved would result in death. Who made the appointment with death the one with the gun, the one with poisoning or someone else?

When we observe making an appointment in that scenario, it can easily be seen that we are in control. Now the opposite would be to look at others who were to die, yet chose to extend their appointment to die.

> [1] In those days Hezekiah was sick and near death. And Isaiah the prophet, the son of Amoz, went to him and said to him, "Thus says the Lord: 'Set your

house in order, for you shall die, and not live.' "

^{2} Then he turned his face toward the wall, and prayed to the Lord, saying,

^{3} "Remember now, O Lord, I pray, how I have walked before You in truth and with a loyal heart, and have done *what was* good in Your sight." And Hezekiah wept bitterly.

^{4} And it happened, before Isaiah had gone out into the middle court, that the word of the Lord came to him, saying,

^{5} "Return and tell Hezekiah the leader of My people, 'Thus says the Lord, the God of David your father: "I have heard your prayer, I have seen your tears; surely I will heal you. On the third day you shall go up to the house of the Lord.

^{6} And I will add to your days fifteen years. I will deliver you and this city from the hand of the king of Assyria; and I will defend this city for My own sake, and for the sake of My servant David." 2 Kings 20:1-6 (NKJV)

The Apostle Paul says he was torn between wanting to go to be with the Lord, which is the better of the two, or staying with the Philippian believers because they needed him.

> [21] For to me, to live *is* Christ, and to die *is* gain.

> [22] But if *I* live on in the flesh, this *will mean* fruit from *my* labor; yet what I shall choose I cannot tell.

> [23] For I am hard pressed between the two, having a desire to depart and be with Christ, *which is* far better.

> [24] Nevertheless to remain in the flesh *is* more needful for you.

> [25] And being confident of this, I know that I shall remain and continue with you all for your progress and joy of faith. Philippians 1:21-25 (NKJV)

Christ, having been once offered, chose to lay His life down at the appointed time of His and the Father's choosing. Satan did not take his life.

[17] Therefore doth my Father love me, because I lay down my life, that I might take it again.

[18] No man taketh it from me, but I lay it down of myself. I have power to lay it down, and I have power to take it again. This commandment have I received of my Father. John 10:17-18 (KJV)

In Hebrews 2:14-15, Christ shared man's mortal nature that by His dying men might be freed from death.

[14] Forasmuch then as the children are partakers of flesh and blood, he also himself likewise took part of the same; that through death he might destroy him that had the power of death, that is, the devil;

[15] And deliver them who through fear of death were all their lifetime subject to bondage.

From the Greek, the original word translated destroy, means to render inoperative; not to be in a position of non-existence. In other words, death cannot lord itself over us.

"For the law of the Spirit of life in Christ Jesus hath made me free from the law of sin and death" (Romans 8:2, NKJV) It appears that Satan and death go hand and hand. Although Satan cannot make one sin, he is the one who influences one to sin, as in the Garden of Eden. We must remember that it was Father God who sent Jesus to destroy death, or to destroy the one who had the power over death. Satan!

Is it possible that John 10:10 is a witness that death is not from God? So many people say the opposite, 'God took him,' is often our response. However, the Bible only records three people who were taken by God and they were alive: Enoch, (Gen 5;24); Elijah, (2 Kings 2:11) and Jesus (Acts 1:9). Has God every taken any one dead? God takes us alive. Selah, pause and think.

> [10] The thief cometh not, but for to steal, and to kill, and to destroy: I am come that they might have life, and that they might have it more abundantly.

Jesus came that we may have more life! Life is to be full and complete, not dead or dying. God the Father and Jesus refer to people who are dead, as being sleep.

[20]But now is Christ risen from the dead, *and* become the first fruits of them that slept. 1 Corinthians 15:20 (KJV)

[11]These things said he: and after that he saith unto them, our friend Lazarus sleepeth; but I go, that I may awake him out of sleep. John 11:11 (KJV)

Eventually, you are going to die. In other words, you actually have an appointment with death and you cannot cancel it. I am certainly not saying that you can avoid death indefinitely. What I am suggesting is that, now that you have accepted and confessed Jesus as the Savior and Lord of your life, there is no longer any need for you to fear death. You now have some control over it. You have control, in the sense that Satan can no longer dictate the length of your days.

Why, because, Jesus has rendered inoperative his power of death over you. The Word says to release those who through fear of death were all their lifetime subject to bondage. Once you recognize that you do have a say in when you die, fear of death will become a thing of the past.

The Word says that death and life are in the power of your tongue, not in the hand of Satan. Death is not just arbitrary; you can and do have a say in when you die. In fact, it is by the words of your mouth that you set "your appointment."

Either you are speaking life to your life - putting off your appointment - or you are speaking death to your life by confessing the negative circumstances you see or have been told.

By agreeing with your negative situation, you give Satan the cooperation he needs to kill you. You are setting your appointment for sooner rather than later. Now, when should you make your appointment with death?

Good question.

Do you remember what the Spirit of the Lord says in Psalm 91:16? "With long life I will satisfy him, and show him My salvation." God says with long life, not short life, not cut off in the prime of your life.

But the Lord does not stop there. The Word of God says you should be satisfied. I say, that if you are not satisfied, then keep on living.

I believe you should not set your appointment until you have enjoyed a long life, have accomplished your purpose and are completely satisfied. If this were not possible, God would be a respecter of persons, demonstrating partiality, because some people live long and satisfying lives, while others die at an early age.

It is unfortunate that most people die long before they are satisfied. They let death tell them when it is time for them to go. They have been robbed, just like the Scripture says, "he comes to steal and kill."

I do not believe the devil has the right to kill a Christian whenever he sees fit, because the Scripture says Jesus came to destroy the works of the devil and to destroy him who had the power of death.

Contrary to popular belief, this idea of having a say in our death is real and could cause many to start shaking their heads. But, when you talk about death, the Bible does have a great deal to say about the subject.

Many have been trained to accept the axiom that death is inevitable and arbitrary. God is the one most often blamed for death. He needed another flower in his garden, so he took sister or brother so-and-so. Most people believe there is really nothing you can do about it. "When your number is up, that's it," is what I have heard many times.

But, the Scriptures say this is not the case. We are not fighting God; we are just denying Satan any right to steal our life.

²³ Hard choice! The desire to break camp here and be with Christ is powerful. Some days I can think of nothing better
Philippians 1:23 (MSG)

Chapter Twelve

Death of Death

"

We are usually afraid to die, because we are afraid we are never coming back", says Dr. Myles Munroe, [3]"but there is a person named Jesus who took on our humanity, shared flesh and blood, and by his <u>death</u> destroyed the power that death had over us. He has freed you and me who were all our lives afraid, scared of death."

"Don't be afraid of death any more. You will see me again. I will see you again, because death has no right to keep us in the grave."

"That's why you must live every day with passion, without fear in your life, pursuing God's will for your life. Do things well, with excellence, with all your might. Don't worry about death. You win either way! If you live or die, you win, because Jesus paid the price. He made death powerless."

When Jesus was talking about Lazarus, he said he is sleeping. He didn't say dead. He was talking future tense with death already destroyed. For so many years, death to man has been defined as dead, the end. But Jesus defines it as sleep.

Jesus told Mary, her brother would live again. She believed he would come back in the last day. Christ corrected her.

In other words, Jesus is saying no matter what day it is, "I am the resurrection". I am carrying about in my body everything required to bring him back. He could have said, "I Am That I Am", but He stated instead that He was the resurrection.

> 25 Jesus said to her, "I am the resurrection and the life. He who believes in Me, though he may die, he shall live.

> 26 And whoever lives and believes in Me shall never die. Do you believe this?" John 11:25-26 (NKJV)

Quoting Dr. Munroe, [3]"Another way he could have said it would be: I am the death that Lazarus died. I have come to destroy death, so that Lazarus and all those who sleep in the grave can come back. Now to show you, Mary, that I can get him now or later, let's go get him now. So Jesus can resurrect now or later. For those of us who have lost loved ones, Jesus is saying later, "I'll resurrect them later" but later is a sure thing. His death took away the power of death."

"Therefore, in order for Christ to destroy death, God must deal with sin. That's the seed of Christ coming to the world as a man. That is what made the destruction of death possible. Dying was not only necessary, but mandatory."

Dr. Myles Munroe debates three questions. "The first question; who killed Jesus? Was it the Romans? Was it the Jews? Was it the soldiers, or the Gentiles?" Isaiah 53:4 says

[4] Surely He has borne our grief and carried our sorrows; yet we esteemed Him stricken, Smitten by God, and afflicted.

The Amplified Bible says it this way:

[4] Surely He has borne our grief (sicknesses, weaknesses, and distresses) and carried our sorrows and

pains [of punishment], yet we [ignorantly] considered Him stricken, smitten, and afflicted by God [as if with leprosy].   Isaiah 53:4 (AMP)

[3]"So who killed Jesus? Read it! God did. God killed himself.   When John was preaching on the beach and he saw Jesus coming down the beach. John stopped preaching, and said of Him, "Look or Behold the lamb of God." The Law God set in motion caused Jesus to die.

"He said that because in those days everybody had their own lamb. They had to bring their own lamb to sacrifice for their sins. But in this case God has provided himself a lamb. No more lambs for your children your cousins, your uncles. God Himself is bringing His own lamb to die for the sins of the world. Therefore, this lamb shall die once and for all."

"The Bible says, He was wounded for our transgressions, He was bruised for our guilt *and* iniquities; the chastisement [needful to obtain] of our peace *and* well-being was upon Him, and with the stripes [that wounded] Him we are healed *and* made whole.

By accepting His sacrifice, you can be healed right now, he has already provided for your healing. Claim it right now! Healing is yours In the name of Jesus."

The second question Dr. Munroe asks is "what killed Jesus? Was it the whip, the nails, the crown, or the spear? The answer: Isaiah 53:6 (NKJV) All we like sheep have gone astray. We have turned, every one, to his own way. And the Lord (the Lord, the Lord) has laid on Him the iniquity of us all. Who laid it on him? The Lord laid it on him."

> [6]All we like sheep have gone astray, we have turned every one to his own way; and the Lord has made to light upon Him the guilt *and* iniquity of us all.
> Isaiah 53:6 (AMP)

[3]"What killed him? The wages of sin is death. Who put it on him? The Lord God Himself put the sins of man on His own Son and He died!"

"The spear did not kill him! The crown did not kill Him. The nails did not kill Him. Sin killed Him."

"The Lord killed him!" Another question that could be asked is what was His goal in His death? Was it as a martyr or for good purpose? Isaiah answers in verse 10."

> [10]Yet it was the will of the Lord to bruise Him; He has put Him to grief *and* made Him sick. When You *and* He make His life an offering for sin [and

He has risen from the dead, in time to come], He shall see His [spiritual] offspring, He shall prolong His days, and the will *and* pleasure of the Lord shall prosper in His hand. Isaiah 53:10 (AMP)

It was the Lord's will to bruise Him; the Lord's will to cause him to suffer. Who's will? It was the Lord's will.

Dr. Munroe continues, "The Lord makes his life a guilt offering. It wasn't Pontius Pilate the governor, it was the Lord. God was solving death."

"The Lord made him an offering for us. He put *Him* to grief, when the Lord made His soul an offering for sin. The Lord made His soul a guilt offering."

"He shall see *His* seed, He shall prolong *His* days, and the pleasure of the LORD shall prosper in His hand, after the Lord kills him. The Lord killed Him for you and me."

The third question, "What was the goal and/or purpose of his death?" Here it is, beginning in Isaiah 53:11:

[11] He shall see the labor of His soul, *and* be satisfied. By His knowledge My righteous Servant shall justify many; For He shall bear their iniquities.

[12] Therefore, I will divide Him a portion with the great, And He shall divide the spoil with the strong, Because He poured out His soul unto death, And He was numbered with the transgressors, and And He bore the sin of many, and made intercession for the transgressors. Isaiah 53:11 (NKJV)

Dr. Munroe says, "After the suffering of His soul He shall see the light of life that means the resurrection, and shall be satisfied. When he goes to death he will see the light of day. He is going to come back to life and when he comes back to life, He will divide the spoils with the strong. Guess who that is? That's the brethren. That's you and me. He gives us what He got."

"Some of the spoils he got were the keys to death, hell and the grave. The word key means to have authority over something. We have authority over hell, because we got authority over sin through His death. We have authority over the grave, because you cannot stay in the grave if you have Him inside your life. You have authority over death, because death cannot keep you in the grave. Therefore, He shares the spoils with us that He gained through His death. He poured out his life unto death and was numbered with the transgressors."

[11] He shall see [the fruit] of the travail of His soul and be satisfied; by His knowledge of Himself [which He possesses and imparts to others] shall My [uncompromisingly] righteous One, My Servant, justify many *and* make many righteous (upright and in right standing with God), for He shall bear their iniquities *and* their guilt [with the consequences, says the Lord]. Isaiah 53:11 (AMP)

"Death got its life when man disobeyed God. In order for God to get rid of death, all he had to do is get rid of, not man, but sin."

"The man did not cause death; sin caused death. But man did cause sin. In order for God to solve death, he must solve sin. If God can solve sin, then he can solve death."

Nicodemus was spiritually dead, when he approached Jesus. This was a death that needed to die within him and a new spirit birthed. In John 3:1, we find the following formula stated by Jesus for spiritual life to be birthed.

[1]There was a man of the Pharisees, named Nicodemus, a ruler of the Jews:

[2] The same came to Jesus by night, and

said unto him, Rabbi, we know that thou art a teacher come from God: for no man can do these miracles that thou doest, except God be with him.

³ Jesus answered and said unto him, Verily, verily, I say unto thee, except a man be born again, he cannot see the kingdom of God.

⁴ Nicodemus saith unto him, how can a man be born when he is old? can he enter the second time into his mother's womb, and be born?

⁵ Jesus answered, Verily, verily, I say unto thee, except a man be born of water and of the Spirit, he cannot enter into the kingdom of God.

⁶ That which is born of the flesh is flesh; and that which is born of the Spirit is spirit.

⁷ Marvel not that I said unto thee, Ye must be born again. John 3:1-7 (KJV)

J. Vernon McGee explains it this way. "God has no program for our old nature, to retrieve it, or improve it, or develop it, or save it. That old nature is to go down into the grave with us. And, if the Lord comes before we go down into the grave, we are to be changed in the twinkling of an eye, which means we will get rid of that old nature. It can never be made obedient to God. "That which is born of the flesh is flesh. That is an axiom. God does not intend to save the flesh at all. This old nature must be replaced by the new nature. The spiritual birth is necessary so that you and I may be given a new nature, friend."

This subject of being born again or rebirthing of our spirit may be seen from the Scripture John 5:24 -25.

> [24] "Most assuredly, I say to you, he who hears My word and believes in Him who sent Me has everlasting life, and shall not come into judgment, but has passed from death into life.
>
> [25] Most assuredly, I say to you, the hour is coming, and now is, when the dead will hear the voice of the Son of God; and those who hear will live. John 5:24-25 (NKJV)

In addition to having a new spirit, we must and will have a new body. Look at it from I Corinthian the fifteenth chapter.

⁴⁰ There are also celestial bodies and terrestrial bodies; but the glory of the celestial is one, and the glory of the terrestrial is another.

⁴¹ There is one glory of the sun, another glory of the moon, and another glory of the stars; for one star differs from another star in glory.

⁴² So also is the resurrection of the dead. The body is sown in corruption, it is raised in incorruption.

⁴³ It is sown in dishonor, it is raised in glory. It is sown in weakness, it is raised in power.

⁴⁴ It is sown a natural body, it is raised a spiritual body. There is a natural body, and there is a spiritual body.

⁴⁵ And so it is written, "The first man Adam became a living being." The last Adam became a life-giving spirit.

⁴⁶ However, the spiritual is not first, but the natural, and afterward the spiritual.

⁴⁷ The first man was of the earth, made

of dust; the second Man is the Lord from heaven.

[48] As was the man of dust, so also are those who are made of dust; and as is the heavenly Man, so also are those who are heavenly.

[49] And as we have borne the image of the man of dust, we shall also bear the image of the heavenly Man. 1 Corinthians 15:40-49 (NKJV)

Paul describes this new body as a mystery. Actually, the mystery of life is greater than the mystery of death. Notice the death of physical death. John 11

[1] Now a certain *man* was sick, *named* Lazarus, of Bethany, the town of Mary and her sister Martha.

[2] (It was *that* Mary which anointed the Lord with ointment, and wiped his feet with her hair, whose brother Lazarus was sick.)

[3] Therefore his sisters sent unto him, saying, Lord, behold, he whom thou lovest is sick.

[4] When Jesus heard *that,* he said, This sickness is not unto death, but for the glory of God, that the Son of God might be glorified thereby.

[5] Now Jesus loved Martha, and her sister, and Lazarus.

[6] When he had heard therefore that he was sick, he abode two days still in the same place where he was.

[7] Then after that saith he to *his* disciples, Let us go into Judaea again.

[8] *His* disciples say unto him, Master, the Jews of late sought to stone thee; and goest thou thither again?

[9] Jesus answered, Are there not twelve hours in the day? If any man walk in the day, he stumbleth not, because he seeth the light of this world.

[10] But if a man walk in the night, he stumbleth, because there is no light in him.

[11] These things said he: and after that he

saith unto them, Our friend Lazarus sleepeth; but I go, that I may awake him out of sleep.

[12] Then said his disciples, Lord, if he sleep, he shall do well.

[13] Howbeit Jesus spake of his death: but they thought that he had spoken of taking of rest in sleep.

[14] Then said Jesus unto them plainly, Lazarus is dead.

[15] And I am glad for your sakes that I was not there, to the intent ye may believe; nevertheless let us go unto him.

[16] Then said Thomas, which is called Didymus, unto his fellow disciples, Let us also go, that we may die with him.

[17] Then when Jesus came, he found that he had *lain* in the grave four days already.

[18] Now Bethany was nigh unto Jerusalem, about fifteen furlongs off:

[19] And many of the Jews came to

Martha and Mary, to comfort them concerning their brother.

[20] Then Martha, as soon as she heard that Jesus was coming, went and met him: but Mary sat *still* in the house.

[21] Then said Martha unto Jesus, Lord, if thou hadst been here, my brother had not died.

[22] But I know, that even now, whatsoever thou wilt ask of God, God will give *it* thee.

[23] Jesus saith unto her, Thy brother shall rise again.

[24] Martha saith unto him, I know that he shall rise again in the resurrection at the last day.

[25] Jesus said unto her, I am the resurrection, and the life: he that believeth in me, though he were dead, yet shall he live:

[26] And whosoever liveth and believeth in me shall never die. Believest thou this? John 11:1-26 (KJV)

You see, although Martha knew from the Old Testament that there would be a resurrection from the dead, she didn't believe that Jesus could help her now.

[4]"Jesus says to her, "Martha, don't you know that I am the resurrection and the life?" If we have Jesus, we have life. "He that believeth in me, though he were dead" is referring to spiritual death. Though a person is spiritually dead, "yet shall he live." Then He looks into the future and says that the one who has trusted Him shall never die. Life begins at the moment a person accepts the Savior. Whosoever lives and believes in Jesus will never die because Jesus has already died for him. That is, he will never die a penal death for his sins. He will never be separated from God. Then Jesus asks the question: "Believest thou this?"

—J. Vernon McGee's Thru The Bible

Therefore, the crisis of Calvary is a simple one. The death of Jesus was not a suicide; it was neither martyrdom, nor was He a political rebel. In the book of Isaiah, Chapter 53 it is very clear. It says that He bore the sin of many and made intercession for the transgressors. What a statement! These statements in Isaiah are very important in our contemporary society, because some people believe that this man Christ died as a martyr.

Isaiah says that this man did not die as a martyr; he did not die as a good rebel. He died to bare the sins of many and became intercessor for the transgressors. His death was for you and for me, so that we would not have to die in sin. That's why if we live in Christ, we live in victory over death.

[20] But now Christ is risen from the dead, *and* has become the first fruits of those who have fallen asleep.

[21] For since by man *came* death, by Man also *came* the resurrection of the dead.

[22] For as in Adam all die, even so in Christ all shall be made alive.

[23] But each one in his own order: Christ the first fruits, afterward those *who are* Christ's at His coming.

[24] Then *comes* the end, when He delivers the kingdom to God the Father, when He puts an end to all rule and all authority and power.

[25] For He must reign till He has put all enemies under His feet.

[26] The last enemy *that* will be destroyed *is* death. 1 Corinthians 15:20-26 (NKJV)

This does not mean that He is going to destroy death. He has already destroyed death. It means the last enemy, after having been victorious over all the enemy's attempts to defeat your conquest and walk with God is now to be destroyed via a resurrection.

[5]Death shall be counter-worked, subverted, and finally overturned. But death cannot be destroyed by there being simply no farther death; death can only be destroyed and annihilated by a general resurrection; if there be no general resurrection, it is most evident that death will still retain his empire. Therefore, the fact that death shall be destroyed assures the fact that there shall be a general resurrection; and this is a proof, also, that after the resurrection there shall be no more death.

—Adam Clarke's Commentary

¹⁹ Behold! I have given you authority and power to trample upon serpents and scorpions, and [physical and mental strength and ability] over all the power that the enemy [possesses]; and nothing shall in any way harm you.

²⁰ Nevertheless, do not rejoice at this, that the spirits are subject to you, but rejoice that your names are enrolled in heaven.

²¹ In that same hour He rejoiced and gloried in the Holy Spirit and said, I thank You, Father, Lord of heaven and earth, that You have concealed these things [relating to salvation] from the wise and understanding and learned, and revealed them to babes (the childish, unskilled, and untaught). Yes, Father, for such was Your gracious will and choice and good pleasure.
Luke 10:19-21 (AMP)

¹⁹ Behold! I have given you authority *and* power to trample upon serpents and scorpions, and [physical and mental strength and ability] over all the power that the enemy [possesses]; and nothing shall in any way harm you.   Luke 10:19 (AMP)

[2]"In order to complete the story of the seventy, Luke describes their return. They came back thrilled and excited. This is the same experience we have when we give out the Word of God, and someone comes to Christ. How glorious we feel! What a lesson for us to remember the words of Jesus, "Rejoice not, that the spirits are subject unto you; but rather rejoice, because your names are written in heaven." When there is success in our ministry, it is His work, not ours."

Death came by sin. Overcome the sin and you overcome the death.

My late pastor, The Rev. Dr. Samuel Farina, describes the death of death as follows:

[1]"Early that first Easter morning a few women came to the tomb of Jesus to mourn...to weep... to anoint a dead body, but they left shouting. "He is risen as He said He would!" They met the risen Lord and sunset turned to sunrise. Good Friday was behind them, Sunday morning had come."

Death has been defeated and the grave has lost all power. Death has lost its sting because we are to look beyond death. We now have the freedom to walk into the vast regions of eternity. The grave cannot hold us down.

"Before the day was over the news spread like wildfire over the entire countryside.

"THE NAZARENE HAS RISEN! THE NAZARENE HAS RISEN!"

The mourners met the risen Lord and they became messengers. Good Friday was behind them, Sunday morning had come!

The disciples met the risen Lord and cowardice turned to courage. Good Friday was behind them, Sunday morning had come!

The two Emmaus disciples met the risen Lord and fear turned to faith. Good Friday was behind them, Sunday morning had come!

Thomas met the risen Lord and doubt turned to discovery. Good Friday was behind him, Sunday morning had come!

The dawn had broken and a new day began. Good Friday was behind them, Sunday morning had come!

The followers of Jesus...who just a few days before turned and ran from Him...and denied Him...and watched Him die...went out as flaming evangelists with a burning message that turned the world upside down and changed the course of history.

They cried out for the whole world to hear: 'The Lord of Glory who was crucified among you is alive! He is risen!' Good Friday was behind them, Sunday morning had come!

And when they preached, their text was taken from the empty tomb. The darkness of Calvary had been pushed back by the rushing light of the

Resurrection. Good Friday was behind them, Sunday morning had come!

God shook the world to its' very foundations when He rolled back that huge stone from in front of the tomb, not to let Jesus out, but to let the world in to see His mighty power. To seal the fact that He has the final word on life and death. The final word on death is that it must give way to life. GOOD FRIDAY IS BEHIND US. SUNDAY MORNING HAS COME!

Christ's resurrection changed Mary from a mourner into a messenger; it changed Thomas from a doubter into a believer, it changed Peter from a denier into a preacher and it changed Paul from a persecutor into a missionary. For early Christians the Easter event became an Easter experience: a powerful life-changing, transforming experience!

Today over 2,000 years later, that Easter event is still the greatest hope in a world filled with fear and confusion!

GOOD FRIDAY IS BEHIND US. SUNDAY MORNING HAS COME!!!

End Notes

[1]Dr. Samuel Farina, "The Death of Death,"
Christian Assembly, April 2005.

[2]WORDsearch Corp. WORDsearch 7,
Jamieson-Fausset-Brown Commentary, July 2002.

[3]Dr. Myles Munroe, his teaching,
The Birth of Death, 2005.

WORDsearch Corp. WORDsearch 7,
[4]J. Vernon McGee's Thru the Bible, July 2002.

[5]Adam Clarke's Commentary, July 2002.

[6]Wesley's Commentary, July 2002.

[7]E. Shuyler English's commentary, July 2002

[8]Easton's Illustrated Dictionary, July 2002

[9]The Late Dr. Richard Houston Holmes, his
    teaching, The Virgin Birth, April 1977

[10]Textbook of Physiology, George Howard Bell,
co written with D. Emslie Smith
and C. R. Paterson 1980, p.553.

[11] WORDsearch Corp. WORDsearch 7,
Mathew Henry commentary, July 2002.

Harriston L. Wilson
may be contacted at:
www.harristonlwilson.com
email: hwilson1700@gmail.com
       hwilson1700@hotmail.com

_____

Death and life are in the power of the
tongue: and they that love it shall eat the
fruit thereof. **Proverbs 18:21 (KJV)**

ABOUT THE AUTHOR

Harriston L. Wilson continues the godly legacy of propagating the gospel as a third generation minister. Sharing the ministerial inheritance of his maternal grandparents and his late mother and father, he has a great love and avid zeal to bring souls into the knowledge of the Lord. Harriston has a Bachelor of Science degree, along with: additional educational studies at The Ohio State University, Theological studies at Moody Bible Institute, and Trinity Lutheran Theological Seminary.

He founded The Bible Rap Session Inc. (B.R.S. Believe, Repent & Be Saved), a ministry which encouraged Believers in churches nationwide to gather for worship, prayer, Scripture studies and discussions. He is also the former manager of The Southern West Virginia Gospel Singers and The Bernard Upshaw singers.

Ordained in the Church of God in Christ, Harriston is an international speaker, retired school teacher, lecturer, and entrepreneur. He currently serves as an elder at Christian Assembly, Columbus, Ohio where he is also a Bible instructor, share group leader, and trustee.

Harriston and his wife Gayle, the proud parents of four children and six grandchildren, join in ministry together in various areas.

Made in the USA
Charleston, SC
18 March 2011